CASEBOOK SERIES

D. H. Lawrence: *Sons and Lovers*

*Casebook Series*

GENERAL EDITOR: A. E. Dyson

Jane Austen: *Emma* DAVID LODGE
T. S. Eliot: *The Waste Land* C. B. COX AND A. HINCHLIFFE
D. H. Lawrence: *Sons and Lovers* GĀMINI SALGĀDO
D. H. Lawrence: '*The Rainbow*' and '*Women in Love*' COLIN
    CLARKE
John Osborne: *Look Back in Anger* J. RUSSELL TAYLOR
Pope: *The Rape of the Lock* JOHN DIXON HUNT
Shakespeare: *Antony and Cleopatra* J. RUSSELL BROWN
Shakespeare: *Hamlet* JOHN JUMP
Shakespeare: *Macbeth* JOHN WAIN
Shakespeare: *The Tempest* D. J. PALMER
Shakespeare: *The Winter's Tale* KENNETH MUIR
Yeats: *Last Poems* JON STALLWORTHY

IN PREPARATION
William Blake: *Songs of Innocence and Experience* MARGARET
    BOTTRALL
Emily Brontë: *Wuthering Heights* MIRIAM ALLOTT
Joseph Conrad: *The Secret Agent* IAN WATT
Charles Dickens: *Bleak House* A. E. DYSON
Donne: *Songs and Sonnets* ANNE RIGHTER
George Eliot: *Middlemarch* PATRICK SWINDEN
T. S. Eliot: *Four Quartets* BERNARD BERGONZI
Henry Fielding: *Tom Jones* NEIL COMPTON
E. M. Forster: *A Passage to India* MALCOLM BRADBURY
Ben Jonson: *Volpone* JONAS BARISH
Keats: *The Odes* G. S. FRASER
Marlowe: *Doctor Faustus* JOHN JUMP
Milton: '*Comus*' and '*Samson Agonistes*' STANLEY FISH
Shakespeare: *Henry IV* Parts I and II G. K. HUNTER
Shakespeare: *Henry V* MICHAEL QUINN
Shakespeare: *Julius Caesar* PETER URE
Shakespeare: *King Lear* FRANK KERMODE
Shakespeare: *Measure for Measure* C. K. STEAD
Shakespeare: *Othello* JOHN WAIN
Shakespeare: *Richard II* NICHOLAS BROOKE
Shakespeare: *The Merchant of Venice* JOHN WILDERS
Tennyson: *In Memoriam* JOHN DIXON HUNT
Virginia Woolf: *To The Lighthouse* MAURICE BEJA
Wordsworth: *Lyrical Ballads* ALUN JONES
Wordsworth: *The Prelude* W. J. HARVEY

# D. H. Lawrence

## *Sons and Lovers*

A CASEBOOK

EDITED BY

GĀMINI SALGĀDO

Aurora Publishers Incorporated

NASHVILLE/LONDON

FIRST PUBLISHED 1969 BY
MACMILLAN AND COMPANY LIMITED
LONDON, ENGLAND

COPYRIGHT © 1970 BY
AURORA PUBLISHERS INCORPORATED
NASHVILLE, TENNESSEE 37219
LIBRARY OF CONGRESS CATALOG CARD NUMBER: 75-127570
STANDARD BOOK NUMBER: 87695-041-1
MANUFACTURED IN THE UNITED STATES OF AMERICA

# CONTENTS

# ACKNOWLEDGEMENTS

Extracts from *Sons and Lovers* and *The Collected Letters of D. H. Lawrence* (the Estate of the late Mrs Frieda Lawrence, Laurence Pollinger Ltd and The Viking Press Inc.); 'E. T.', *D. H. Lawrence: A Personal Record* (the Executors of the E. T. (Jessie Chambers) Estate, and Jonathan Cape Ltd); A. B. Kuttner, 'A Freudian Appreciation', from *Psychoanalytic Review*, July 1916; John Middleton Murry, *Son of Woman* (The Society of Authors as the literary representative of the Estate of the late John Middleton Murry); Mark Schorer, 'Technique as Discovery', from *Hudson Review*, 1 i (Spring 1948) (© Mark Schorer 1966); Dorothy Van Ghent, 'On *Sons and Lovers*', from *The English Novel: Form and Function* (Holt, Rinehart and Winston Inc., Publishers, New York; © Dorothy Van Ghent 1953); Seymour Betsky, 'Rhythm and Theme in *Sons and Lovers*', from *The Achievement of D. H. Lawrence*, ed. and with an introduction by Frederick J. Hoffman and Harry T. Moore (© the University of Oklahoma Press 1953); Frank O'Connor, *The Mirror in the Roadway* (A. D. Peters & Co. and Miss Cyrilly Abels; © 1955, 1956); Graham Hough, *The Dark Sun* (The Macmillan Company and Gerald Duckworth & Co. Ltd; © Graham Hough 1957); Simon O. Lesser, *Fiction and the Unconscious* (Peter Owen Ltd and the Beacon Press; © Simon O. Lesser 1957); David Daiches, *The Novel and the Modern World* (The University of Chicago Press); Eliseo Vivas, *D. H. Lawrence: The Failure and Triumph of Art* (George Allen & Unwin Ltd and Northwestern University Press); Maurice Beebe, *Ivory Towers and Sacred Founts* (New York University Press); H. M. Daleski, *The Forked Flame* (Faber & Faber Ltd and Northwestern University Press); Dr Keith Sagar, *The Art of D. H. Lawrence* (Cambridge University Press); Laurence Lerner, *The Truthtellers* (Chatto & Windus Ltd).

The Editor wishes to thank Jane Snelling for helping with the proof-reading.

# GENERAL EDITOR'S PREFACE

EACH of this series of Casebooks concerns either one well-known and influential work of literature or two or three closely linked works. The main section consists of critical readings, mostly modern, brought together from journals and books. A selection of reviews and comments by the author's contemporaries is also included, and sometimes comments from the author himself. The Editor's Introduction charts the reputation of the work from its first appearance until the present time.

What is the purpose of such a collection? Chiefly, to assist reading. Our first response to literature may be, or seem to be, 'personal'. Certain qualities of vigour, profundity, beauty or 'truth to experience' strike us, and the work gains a foothold in our mind. Later, an isolated phrase or passage may return to haunt or illuminate. Where did we hear that? we wonder – it could scarcely be better put.

In these and similar ways appreciation begins, but major literature prompts to very much more. There are certain facts we need to know if we are to understand properly. Who were the author's original readers, and what assumptions did he share with them? What was his theory of literature? Was he committed to a particular historical situation, or to a set of beliefs? We need historians as well as critics to help us with this. But there are also more purely literary factors to take account of: the work's structure and rhetoric; its symbols and archetypes; its tone, genre and texture; its use of language; the words on the page. In all these matters critics can inform and enrich our individual responses by offering imaginative recreations of their own.

For the life of a book is not, after all, merely 'personal'; it is more like a tripartite dialogue, between a writer living 'then', a reader living 'now', and whatever forces of survival and honour link the two. Criticism is the public manifestation of this dialogue, a witness to the continuing power of literature to arouse and excite. It illuminates the possibilities and rewards of the dialogue, pushing 'interpretation' as far forward as it can go.

And here, indeed, is the rub: how far can it go? Where does 'interpretation' end and nonsense begin? Why is one interpretation superior to another, and why does each age need to interpret for itself? The critic knows that his insights have value only in so far as they serve the text, and that he must take account of views sharply differing from his own. He knows that his own writing will be judged as well as the work he writes about, so that he cannot simply assert inner illumination or a differing taste.

The critical forum is a place of vigorous conflict and disagreement, but there is nothing in this to cause dismay. What is attested is the complexity of human experience and the richness of literature, not any chaos or relativity of taste. A critic is better seen, no doubt, as an explorer than as an 'authority', but explorers ought to be, and usually are, well equipped. The effect of good criticism is to convince us of what C. S. Lewis called 'the enormous extension of our being which we owe to authors'. A Casebook will be justified only if it helps to promote the same end.

A single volume can represent no more than a small selection of critical opinions. Some critics have been excluded for reasons of space, and it is hoped that readers will follow up the further suggestions in the Select Bibliography. Other contributions have been severed from their original context, to which some readers may wish to return. Indeed, if they take a hint from the critics represented here, they certainly will.

A. E. DYSON

# INTRODUCTION

*Sons and Lovers* was not the first novel that Lawrence wrote (*The White Peacock* and *The Trespasser* precede it), but, except for the masterly assurance with which it is done, it could very easily have been. By this I mean that it has many of the marks of the novel that the novelist has to get out of his system in order to come to grips with his real imaginative vision. To say this could be misleading, since it suggests that what Lawrence deals with in *Sons and Lovers* is not a part of his 'real' vision, when almost the exact opposite is true. Nevertheless those who see the height of Lawrence's achievement in *The Rainbow* and *Women in Love* can see *Sons and Lovers*, in retrospect, as the inescapable condition of that achievement. 'One sheds one's sicknesses in books' – to none of his novels are Lawrence's own words more applicable.

All Lawrence's novels are more or less autobiographical in the sense that they deal with the events as well as the emotions of his own life, but *Sons and Lovers* is the most autobiographical even of Lawrence's novels. The first draft of the book was called 'Paul Morel' and the degree of the author's involvement with the central character has led some critics (mistakenly I think) to read the book as an apologia rather than a novel. The chief characters and the central situation are quite clearly taken from Lawrence's own early life. It will come as no surprise to readers of *Sons and Lovers* to learn that Lawrence senior was a miner in Eastwood (on the Nottinghamshire–Derbyshire border), uncouth and often drunk, with no formal education, but a certain openness of nature and zest for life which made him popular among his workmates. This man married a woman who was in many ways his direct opposite. To begin with, she was a crucial rung above him on the social ladder, belonging to the shabby-genteel lower-middle class. Her religious outlook was that of a narrow Congregation-alism ('hymn-singing tin-chapel pietism' as a hostile critic called it) quite at odds with his free-and-easy hedonism. While Arthur Lawrence was barely literate, Lydia Beardsall, whom he married, had been a schoolteacher and had pretensions to middle-class respectability which her husband despised when he bothered to take notice of them. The essentially masculine social life of a Midland mining village into which he settled with genial accept-ance seemed to her sterile and constricting beyond endurance. Deprived of the resources to which her upbringing had ac-customed her and soon disillusioned in those which her married life had seemed to offer, she tried with desperate resolution to realize vicariously through her children those ideals of success, happiness and social esteem of which she herself had been thwarted. Small wonder, then, that her married life was a con-tinual battle with her husband, relieved by the solace she found in her children, especially her sons, and ending only with her death by cancer after more than twenty-five years of married misery. Her death, which occurred at the same time as the publication of *The White Peacock*, Lawrence's first novel, was the first of three major crises in Lawrence's life, the other two being his elopement with Frieda Weekley in 1912 and his experiences as a suspected civilian (Frieda was German) during the First World War.

If the domestic background of the Morels is drawn from life, so to a very great extent is that of the Leivers and Willey Farm. A good deal of criticism has concerned itself with the question of whether Lawrence was 'fair' in his portrayal of the real-life counterparts of Miriam, Mr and Mrs Morel, and the rest. The best and best-known example of this sort of criticism is *D. H. Lawrence: A Personal Record*, by Jessie Chambers, the girl portrayed in the novel as 'Miriam'. (Her book was originally published under the initials 'E.T.', standing for the eponymous heroine of an unpublished novel 'Eunice Temple' by Jessie Chambers.) On all the available evidence (which includes not only her own account and letters to Lawrence, but reminiscences by friends and relations), Jessie Chambers was a very remarkable person in her own right. Sharing Lawrence's intelligence and his enormous youthful appetite for literature and ideas, she seems also to have had the capacity to bring out in him that almost subcutaneous sensitivity to experience which is the hallmark of Lawrence's writing. Much of *A Personal Record* is a moving account of the real-life relationship between Lawrence and Miss Chambers, and it ends by showing how, under the dominant influence of his mother, Lawrence distorted the actual relationship between himself and the girl. It is impossible not to respond to the dignity and candour of Jessie Chambers' story or to remain unmoved by the sense of betrayal which vibrates through it. It is quite understandable that the reader's first reaction on reading Jessie Chambers' memoir and the other evidence relating to the triangular relationship between Lawrence, his mother and Jessie should be very similar to Jessie's own. We feel that Lawrence has not really played fair by the girl, that she wasn't really like that at all, that *it* wasn't really like that at all. Indeed, the *Athenaeum* reviewer makes just this point. But it is necessary to try to distinguish between the demands we may fairly make of a novelist as novelist from those we may make of him as an individual. Lawrence's responsibilities in his private relationship are one thing, his responsibilities as a novelist are quite another. To equate the two is to confuse the truth of history with the truth of fiction. To put it slightly differently, the 'truth' that the novelist attempts to portray for us has to be judged in terms of the vividness, internal consistency and inclusiveness of his vision rather than by its accuracy as a chronicle of what in fact happened at a given time and place. There is a perfectly proper sense in which the question of whether the author is 'fair' to his characters may be asked of *Sons and Lovers*, as it may be asked of any novel. But the answer to it involves an account of the characters in their relation to each other and the fictional world they inhabit, and of the author's attitude to them *as it appears in the details of the novel*, not a measuring-off of the fictional characters against their real-life counterparts. The latter may tell us something about the novelist, but nothing of value about the novel. It cannot even tell us *how* the novel fails (where it does), only *why* the novelist fails. 'Never trust the artist, trust the tale.'

From the kind of criticism which sees the novel as illuminating the private life of the author it is a short but important step to that which sees it as illuminating the private life of us all. Almost as soon as *Sons and Lovers* appeared there were critics who saw in it a startling endorsement of Freudian theories about the Oedipus complex. Lawrence had not read Freud when he wrote *Sons and Lovers* (though while he was working on the novel he did hear of Freud's theories from Frieda, who herself came to know of them through meeting a young Austrian disciple of Freud). Of course this does not weaken the case of those who saw a dramatization of Freudian theory in the novel, but rather strengthens it. Practised with a proper regard for the unity and texture of the novel itself, this kind of approach can yield insights that would not otherwise be easily obtained, as Simon Lesser shows. But there seem to be at least two dangers to which this sort of criticism is unusually susceptible. First, it often ignores the palpable surface of the novel, what is really *there*, in its eagerness to get at what is *really* there. It smooths awkward details in its effort to cut the novel into the size and shape that fits the theory. Secondly, it tends to use the theory as a criterion by which to judge the value of the novel (that is, the more the novel endorses the theory, the better it is). Lawrence's own objections to the psycho-analytic approach were rather different, though they have some points of contact with the sort of objections I have listed. The psycho-analysing critics, he felt, falsified the living truths of the novel in the name of the half-truths of intellectual schematizing. Nevertheless *Sons and Lovers* continues to invite this kind of critical approach rather more than most other novels (a recent full-length study by an American critic is called *Oedipus in Nottingham*) and this fact is an interesting and important clue to one of the sources of its power. Even critics who are not wholly committed to a 'psycho-analytic' theory of criticism have been able to make perceptive comments on aspects of *Sons and Lovers* by looking at it in the light of what psycho-analysis has to say about repression and sublimation, about the dark and devious workings of our unconscious desires and how they affect the everyday surface of our lives. It is, however, important to distinguish between the psycho-analytic criticism which honestly tries to relate the 'manifest' content (texture, character, plot) of the novel to its 'latent' meaning, and that which merely reduces the novel to a verbalization of its author's psychological inadequacies. Only the former is the proper concern of literary criticism.

An aspect of the novel which critics were unanimous in responding to with enthusiasm from the outset was Lawrence's power to evoke the feel and tempo of life in the Midlands during the early years of this century, when the old agricultural England lived in an uneasy truce with the early phase of advancing industrialization. Even the critic who remarked that 'It is hard to see why the author chose the coal fields of Derbyshire as his setting, and for his hero the son of a miner' went on to say that 'As to the general background, there can be no question that the writer has his eye on the object.' As far back as 1913 Lawrence did for the novel what John Osborne was to do for the theatre more than forty years later. He portrayed the life and background of a part of English society largely ignored by imaginative writers, without patronizing humour or romantic identification and with a resolutely blind eye for the merely picturesque. In so doing he pushed back the frontiers of fiction not only geographically and socially, but imaginatively. And that remains an important achievement, whatever our estimate of later 'regional' novelists of the North and Midlands who have tried to follow the trail which Lawrence blazed.

As a *Bildungsroman*, the novel which traces the growth and development of a talented hero from childhood to maturity, *Sons and Lovers* is a distinguished example of a typically post-Romantic subdivision within the novel. A comparison of Lawrence's novel with Joyce's *Portrait of the Artist as a Young Man* will tell us a great deal, not only about these two writers, but also about many of the dilemmas facing the artist, particularly if he springs from a provincial rather than a metropolitan background. But, though the fact that Paul Morel is an artist is important for an understanding of the novel, we do not find here the single-minded pursuit of a destiny early and clearly comprehended which is the outstanding feature of Joyce's novel. This comparative obliquity of the artist-as-hero theme may account for the fact that critics did not begin to explore it till comparatively recently.

*Sons and Lovers*, in the fifty-odd years since its first publication, has attracted a very great deal of good criticism drawing on very different analytic techniques and assumptions of value. This volume is intended, among other things, to give some indication of the range and variety of this criticism, and to suggest by implication something of the many-layered richness of the book which provoked it.

The variety of critical approaches is not only stimulating in itself but should be a useful corrective to any lingering notion that there is only one 'correct' way to read a novel, a notion which is probably inapplicable even to such a comparatively simple narrative structure as The House that Jack Built. (This does not mean that there are no 'bad' readings of a novel; but I doubt whether any critical method will by itself prevent us from being lazy, or irresponsible or dishonest with ourselves.)

I have tried not to include anything which did not seem to me either interesting or true, though I have interpreted both the operative words very liberally indeed.

The reader will make his own judgement of the validity and helpfulness of the various viewpoints represented here. Some indication of their range can be gathered by comparing, for instance, essays which place the emphasis on some of the formal resources of the novel – imagery, structure, rhythm and so on – with those which attempt to set the novel within a wider tradition, whether historical or in terms of an individual reshaping of a common theme. In the first group I would place the essays by Dorothy Van Ghent, David Daiches and Seymour Betsky, in the second those by Frank O'Connor and Maurice Beebe. Another possible contrast is between critics such as Keith Sagar, whose main concern is to see *Sons and Lovers* as an independent and distinctive achievement, and those such as H. M. Daleski who try to trace within the novel a particular phase of a theme (the male/female duality) which they take to be pervasive in Lawrence. Apart from Simon Lesser, whose contribution has already been referred to, two earlier critiques with a Freudian bias, by Alfred Booth Kuttner, are also included. But these rough-and-ready distinctions are useful, if at all, only in indicating the broad area of the critic's interest; they are certainly not intended as directions on how to 'take' the criticism, and to prevent them from being so taken I have made them as vague as I usefully could.

The defects of the novel are perhaps as evident as its virtues and have certainly not lacked critics to point them out, and Mark Schorer's essay included here is still, after twenty years, one of the most stimulating adverse critiques. But in the end it is not critical charity but mere critical justice which prompts agreement with one of the book's earliest reviewers who wrote that 'the sum of its defects is astonishingly large, but we only note it when they are weighed against the sum of its own qualities'.

GĀMINI SALGĀDO

# PART ONE

# Extracts from Letters

# FROM LAWRENCE'S LETTERS
# (1910-16)

*To Sydney S. Pawling, 18 October 1910*

... I will give you – with no intermediary this time – my third novel, 'Paul Morel' [the early title of *Sons and Lovers*], which is plotted out very interestingly (to me), and about one-eighth of which is written. 'Paul Morel' will be a novel – not a florid prose poem,* or a decorated idyll running to seed in realism:† but a restrained, somewhat impersonal novel. It interests me very much.

*To Rachel Annand Taylor, 3 December 1910*

I have been at home now ten days. My mother is very near the end.‡ Today I have been to Leicester. I did not get home till half past nine. Then I ran upstairs. Oh she was very bad. The pains had been again.

'Oh my dear' I said, 'is it the pains?'

'Not pain now – Oh the weariness' she moaned, so that I could hardly hear her. I wish she could die tonight.

My sister and I do all the nursing. My sister is only 22. I sit upstairs hours and hours till I wonder if ever it were true that I was at London. I seem to have died since, and that is an old life, dreamy.

I will tell you. My mother was a clever, ironical delicately moulded woman of good, old burgher descent. She married below her. My father was dark, ruddy, with a fine laugh. He is a

---

* Referring to *The Trespasser?*
† Referring to *The White Peacock?*
‡ Lawrence's mother died on 9 December 1910.

coal miner. He was one of the sanguine temperament, warm and hearty, but unstable: he lacked principle, as my mother would have said. He deceived her and lied to her. She despised him – he drank.

Their marriage life has been one carnal, bloody fight. I was born hating my father: as early as ever I can remember, I shivered with horror when he touched me. He was very bad before I was born.

This has been a kind of bond between me and my mother. We have loved each other, almost with a husband and wife love, as well as filial and maternal. We know each other by instinct. She said to my aunt – about me:

'But it has been different with him. He has seemed to be part of me.' – And that is the real case. We have been like one, so sensitive to each other that we never needed words. It has been rather terrible and has made me, in some respects, abnormal.

I think this peculiar fusion of soul (don't think me highfalutin) never comes twice in a life-time – it doesn't seem natural. When it comes it seems to distribute one's consciousness far abroad from oneself, and one understands! I think no one has got 'Understanding' except through love. Now my mother is nearly dead, and I don't quite know how I am.

I have been to Leicester today, I have met a girl* who has always been warm for me – like a sunny happy day – and I've gone and asked her to marry me: in the train, quite unpremeditated, between Rothley and Quorn – she lives at Quorn. When I think of her I feel happy with a sort of warm radiation – she is big and dark and handsome. There were five other people in the carriage. Then when I think of my mother: – if you've ever put your hand round the bowl of a champagne glass and squeezed it and wondered how near it is to crushing-in and the wine all going through your fingers – that's how my heart feels – like the champagne glass. There is no hostility between the warm happiness and the crush of misery: but one is concentrated in my chest, and one is diffuse – a suffusion, vague.

* Louie Burrows, according to Jessie Chambers, one of the models for Clara Dawes.

Muriel [Jessie Chambers] is the girl I have broken with. She loves me to madness, and demands the soul of me. I have been cruel to her, and wronged her, but I did not know.

Nobody can have the soul of me. My mother has had it, and nobody can have it again. Nobody can come into my very self again, and breathe me like an atmosphere. Don't say I am hasty this time – I know. Louie – whom I wish I could marry the day after the funeral – she would never demand to drink me up and have me. She loves me – but it is a fine, warm, healthy, natural love – not like Jane Eyre, who is Muriel, but like – say Rhoda Fleming or a commoner Anna Karenina. She will never plunge her hands through my blood and feel for my soul, and make me set my teeth and shiver and fight away. Ugh – I have done well – and cruelly – tonight.

I look at my father – he is like a cinder. It is very terrible, mis-marriage.

*To Edward Garnett, 6 March 1912*

. . . By the way, would you care to see the MS of the colliery novel, when it is finished, before it goes to Wm H. [Heinemann, the publisher]. I have done two thirds or more. . . . Here, in this ugly hell, the men are *most* happy. They sing, they drink, they rejoice in the land. There were more 'drunks' run-in from the Crown and the Drum here last week-end, than ever since Shire-brook was Shirebrook. Yesterday I was in Worksop. It is simply snyed with pals. Every blessed place was full of men, in the larkiest of spirits. I went in the Golden Crown and a couple of other places. They were betting like steam on skittles – the 'seconds' had capfuls of money. There is some life up here this week, I can tell you. Everywhere you go, crowds and crowds of men, not unhappy, as they usually are.

*To Edward Garnett, 3 April 1912*

. . . I shall finish my colliery novel this week – the first draft. It'll want a bit of revising. It's by far the best thing I've done.

EDITOR'S NOTE

*Early in June 1912 'Paul Morel' was submitted to William Heinemann, who rejected it. The novel was then submitted to Duckworth at the instigation of Edward Garnett, who also suggested a number of alterations.*

To Edward Garnett, 25 July 1912

I got 'Paul Morel' this morning, and the list of notes from Duckworth. The latter are awfully nice and detailed. What a Trojan of energy and conscientiousness you are! I'm going to slave like a Turk at the novel – see if I won't do you credit. I begin in earnest tomorrow – having spent the day in thought (?) . . . Here, in this tiny savage little place, F. [Frieda Weekley] and I have got awfully wild. I loathe the idea of England, and its enervation and misty miserable modernness. I don't want to go back to town and civilisation. I want to rough it and scramble through free, free. I *don't* want to be tied down. And I can live on a tiny bit. I shan't let F. leave me, if I can help it. I feel I've got a mate and I'll fight tooth and claw to keep her. She says I'm reverting, but I'm not – I'm only coming out wholesome and myself. Say I'm right, and I ought to be always common. I *loathe* 'Paul Morel'. F. sends love.
[P.S.] I'll do you credit with that novel, if I can.

To A. W. McLeod, September 1912

. . . 'Paul Morel' is better than *The White Peacock* or *The Trespasser*. I'm inwardly very proud of it, though I haven't yet licked it into form – am still at that labour of love. Heinemann refused it because he was cross with me for going to Duckworth – refused it on grounds of its indecency, if you please.

To Edward Garnett, 14 November 1912

I hasten to tell you I sent the MS of the 'Paul Morel' novel to Duckworth registered, yesterday. And I want to defend it, quick. I wrote it again, pruning it and shaping it and filling it in. I tell you it has got form – *form*: haven't I made it patiently, out of sweat as well as blood. It follows this idea: a woman of character and refinement goes into the lower class, and has no satisfaction in her own life. She has had a passion for her husband, so the children are born of passion, and have heaps of vitality. But as her sons grow up she selects them as lovers – first the eldest, then the second. These sons are *urged* into life by their reciprocal love of their mother – urged on and on. But when they come to manhood, they can't love, because their mother is the strongest power in their lives, and holds them. . . . As soon as the young men come into contact with women, there's a split. William gives his sex to a fribble, and his mother holds his soul. But the split kills him, because he doesn't know where he is. The next son gets a woman who fights for his soul – fights his mother. The son loves the mother – all the sons hate and are jealous of the father. The battle goes on between the mother and the girl, with the son as object. The mother gradually proves stronger, because of the tie of blood. The son decides to leave his soul in his mother's hands, and, like his elder brother go for passion. He gets passion. Then the split begins to tell again. But, almost unconsciously, the mother realises what is the matter, and begins to die. The son casts off his mistress, attends to his mother dying. He is left in the end naked of everything, with the drift towards death.

It is a great tragedy, and I tell you that I have written a great book. It's the tragedy of thousands of young men in England – it may even be Bunny's* tragedy. I think it was Ruskin's, and men like him. – Now tell me if I haven't worked out my theme, like life, but always my theme. Read my novel. It's a great novel. If *you* can't see the development – which is slow, like growth – I can.

*To A. W. McLeod [postmark 26 April 1913]*

Pray to your gods for me that *Sons and Lovers* shall succeed. People should begin to take me seriously now. And I do so break

* David Garnett, the novelist and son of Edward.

my heart over England when I read *The New Machiavelli*. And I am so sure that only through a readjustment between men and women, and a making free and healthy of this sex, will she get out of her present atrophy. Oh, Lord, and if I don't 'subdue my art to a metaphysic,' as somebody very beautifully said of Hardy, I do write because I want folk – English folk – to alter, and have more sense.

*To Edward Garnett, 19 May 1913*

The copy of *Sons and Lovers* has just come – I am fearfully proud of it. I reckon it is quite a great book. I shall not write quite in that style any more. It's the end of my youthful period. Thanks a hundred times.

*To A. W. McLeod, 21 October 1913*

... You must continue to believe in me – I don't mean in my talent only – because I depend on you a bit. One doesn't know, till one is a bit at odds with the world, how much one's friends who believe in one rather generously, mean to one. I felt you had gone off from me a bit, because of *Sons and Lovers*. But one sheds one's sicknesses in books – repeats and presents again one's emotions, to be master of them.

*To Edward Garnett, 30 December 1913*

I shan't write in the same manner as *Sons and Lovers* again, I think – in that hard, violent style full of sensation and presentation.

*To Barbara Low, 11 September 1916*

I hated the *Psychoanalysis* [*sic*] *Review* of *Sons and Lovers*.* You know I think 'complexes' are vicious half-statements of the

* This may refer to A. B. Kuttner's critical article reprinted on pp. 69–94 of the present volume. G.S.

Freudians: sort of can't see wood for trees. When you've said *Mutter*-complex, you've said nothing – no more than if you called hysteria a nervous disease. Hysteria isn't nerves, a complex is not simply a sex relation: far from it. – My poor book: it was, as art, a fairly complete truth: so they carve a half lie out of it, and say 'Voilà.' Swine! . . .

# FROM FRIEDA
# LAWRENCE'S LETTERS

*To Edward Garnett* [?*September 1912*]

. . . I think L. quite missed the point in 'Paul Morel.' He really loved his mother more than anybody, even with his other women, real love, sort of Oedipus; his mother must have been adorable. He is writing P. M. again, reads bits to me and we fight like blazes over it, he is so often beside the point. . . .

*To Edward Garnett* [?*September 1912*]

. . . I also feel as if I ought to say something about L.'s formlessness. I don't think he has no form. I used to. But now I think anybody must see in 'Paul Morel' the hang of it. The mother is really the thread, the domineering note. I think the honesty, the vividness of a book suffers if you subject it to form. I have heard so much about 'form' with Ernest; why are you English so keen on it? Their own form wants smashing in almost any direction, but they can't come out of their snail house. I know it is so much safer. That's what I love Lawrence for, that he is so plucky and honest in his work. I quite firmly believe that L. is quite great in spite of his 'gaps'. Look at the vividness of his stuff, it knocks you down, I think. It is perhaps too 'intimate', comes too close, but I believe that is youth. . . . Don't think I am impudent to say all this, but I feel quite responsible for 'Paul'. I wrote little female bits and lived it over in my own heart. . . .

*To Harry T. Moore, 30 January 1951*

. . . L. felt unhappy about hurting ['Miriam's'] feelings. She *was* deeply hurt. She was the 'sacred love,' you know the old split of sacred and profane. She tries to defend her position by insisting on the 'purity', which gives the show away. Humanly as a whole she wasn't the person his mother was, so the best horse won. She bored me in the end. There was some correspondence between L. and her about the book, but when she had read it, she never wrote again. In writing about her, he had to find out impersonally what was wrong in their relationship, when so much had been good. But what was insufficient in her, how could she admit or even see it. . . .

*To Harry T. Moore, 14 January 1955*

. . . I never told you about my friend, a young Austrian doctor who had worked with Freud and who revolutionised my life with Freud. Through him and then through me Lawrence knew about Freud. . . .

# ORIGINAL FOREWORD TO
## *SONS AND LOVERS* (1913)

*To Edward Garnett*

John, the beloved disciple, says, 'The Word was made Flesh'.
But why should he turn things round? The women simply go on
bearing talkative sons, as an answer. 'The Flesh was made Word.'

For what was Christ? He was Word, or He became Word.
What remains of Him? No flesh remains on earth, from Christ;
perhaps some carpentry He shaped with His hands retains some-
where His flesh-print; and then His word, like His carpentry
just the object that His flesh produced, is the rest. He is Word.
And the Father was Flesh. For even if it were by the Holy Ghost
His spirit were begotten, yet flesh cometh only out of flesh. So
the Holy Ghost must either have been, or have borne from the
Father, at least one grain of flesh. The Father was Flesh – and the
Son, who in Himself was finite and had form, become Word.
For form is the uttered Word, and the Son is the Flesh as it
utters the Word, but the unutterable Flesh is the Father.

And the Word is not spoken by the Father, who is Flesh,
forever unquestioned and unanswerable, but by the Son. Adam
was the first Christ: not the Word made Flesh, but the Flesh
made Word. Out of the Flesh cometh the Word, and the Word
is finite, as a piece of carpentry, and hath an end. But the Flesh
is infinite and has no end. Out of the Flesh cometh the Word,
which blossoms for a moment and is no more. Out of the Flesh
hath come every Word, and in the Flesh lies every Word that
will be uttered. The Father is the Flesh, the eternal and unquestionable, the law-giver but not the law; whereas the Son is the
mouth. And each law is a fabric that must crumble away, and the
Word is a graven image that is worn down, and forsaken, like
the Sphinx in the desert.

*We* are the Word, we are not the Flesh. The Flesh is beyond us. And when we love our neighbour as ourself, we love that word, our neighbour, and not that flesh. For that Flesh is not our neighbour, it is the Father, which is in Heaven, and forever beyond our knowledge. We are the Word, we know the Word, and the Word alone is ours. When we say 'I', we mean 'The Word I am'. This flesh I am is beyond me.

So that if we love our neighbour, we love that Word, our neighbour, and we hate that Lie, our neighbour, which is a deformity. With that Flesh, our neighbour, We, the Word-Utterer, have nothing to do. For the Son is not greater than the Father. And if we love and subserve that Flesh, our neighbour, which is the Father, it is only by denying and desecrating the Father in ourselves. For the Father is the Almighty. The Flesh will feel no pain that is not upon itself, and will know no hurt but its own destruction. But no man can destroy the Almighty, yet he can deny Him. And pain is a denial of the Father. If then we feel the pain and suffering of our neighbour's flesh, we are putting destruction upon our own flesh, which is to deny and make wrathful the Father. Which we have done. For in loving our neighbour, the Flesh, as ourself, we have said, 'There is no Father, there is only the Word.' For it is the Word hath charity, not the Flesh. And it is the Word that answereth the cry of the Word. But if the Word, hearing a cry, shall say, 'My flesh is destroyed, the bone melteth away', that is to blaspheme the Father. For the Word is but fabric builded of the Flesh. And when the fabric is finished, then shall the Flesh enjoy it in its hour.

But we have said, 'Within this fabric of the Word the Flesh is held.' And so, the Son has usurped the Father. And so, the Father, which is the Flesh, withdraws from us, and the Word stands in ruins, as Nineveh and Egypt are dead words on the plains, whence the Flesh has withdrawn itself. For the lesser cannot contain the greater, nor the Son contain the Father, but he is of the Father.

And it is upon the head of that nation that shall deny the Father. For the Flesh will depart from that collective Word, the nation, and that great nation shall remain as a Word in ruin, its own monument.

For who shall say, 'No child shall be born of me and my wife. I, the Word, have said it?' And who shall say – 'That woman whom my flesh, in its unquestionable sincerity, cleaveth toward, shall not come unto my flesh. But my Word shall come unto her. I, the Word have said it?' That is to usurp the flesh of my neighbour, and hold governance over it by the word. And who shall say, 'That woman shall be Flesh of my Flesh. I, the Word, have said it?' For either the woman is Flesh of my Flesh, or she is not, and the Word altereth nothing, but can only submit or deny.

And when we burned the heretic at the stake, then did we love that Word, our neighbour, and hate that lie, the heretic. But we did also deny the Father, and say, 'There is only Word'. And when we suffer in our flesh the pangs of those that hunger, then we do deny the Flesh, and say, it is not. For the Flesh suffereth not from the hunger of the neighbour, but only from its own hunger. But the Word loveth its neighbour, and shall answer to the cry of the Word, 'It is just, what thou askest'. For the Word hath neither passion nor pain, but lives and moves in equity. It has charity, which we call love. But only the Flesh has love, for that is the Father, and in love he begets us all, of love are we begotten. But it was spoken, 'They shall be one Flesh'. Thus did the Word usurp the Father, saying, 'I unite you one flesh'. Whereas the Word can but conform. For the twain are one flesh, whether the Word speak or not. And if they be not one twain, then the Word can never make them so, for the Flesh is not contained in the Word, but the Word in the Flesh. But if a man shall say, 'This woman is flesh of my flesh', let him see to it that he be not blaspheming the Father. For the woman is not flesh of his flesh, by the bidding of the Word; but it is of the Father. And if he take a woman, saying in the arrogance of the Word, 'The flesh of that woman is goodly', then he has said, 'The flesh of that woman is goodly as a servant unto the Word, which is me,' and so hath blasphemed the Father, by which he has his being, and she hath her being. And the Flesh shall forsake these two, they shall be fabric of Word. And their race shall perish.

But if in my passion I slay my neighbour, it is no sin of mine, but it is his sin, for he should not have permitted me. But if my Word shall decide and decree that my neighbour die, then that is sin, for the Word destroyeth the Flesh, the Son blasphemeth the Father. And yet, if a man hath denied his Flesh, saying, 'I, the Word, have dominion over the flesh of my neighbour', then shall the Flesh, his neighbour, slay him in self-defence. For a man may hire my Word, which is the utterance of my flesh, which is my work. But my Flesh is the Father, which is before the Son.

And so it was written: 'The Word was made Flesh', then, as corollary, 'And of the Flesh was made Flesh-of-the-Flesh, woman.' This is again backward, and because the Son, struggling to utter the Word, took for his God the accomplishment of his work, the Uttered Word. Out of his flesh the Word had to come, and the flesh was difficult and unfathomed, so it was called the servant. And the servant of the servant was woman. So the Son arranged it, because he took for his God his own work when it should be accomplished: as if a carpenter called the chair he struggled with but had not yet made, God. But the Chair is not a god, it is only a rigid image. So is the Word a rigid image, parallel of the chair. And so the end having been chosen for the beginning, the whole chronology is upside-down: the Word created Man, and Man lay down and gave birth to Woman. Whereas we know the Woman lay in travail, and gave birth to Man, who in his hour uttered his word.

It is as if a bit of apple-blossom stood for God in his Wonder, the apple was the Son, as being something more gross but still wonderful, while the pip that comes out of the apple, like Adam's rib, is the mere secondary produce, that is spat out, and which, if it falls to the ground, just happens to start the process of apple-tree going again. But the little pip that one spits out has in it all the blossom and apples, as well as all the tree, the leaves, the perfume, the drops of gum, and heaven knows what else that we never see, contained by miracle in its bit of white flesh: and the tree, the leaves, the flowers themselves, and the apple are only amplifications of this little seed, spent: which never has amplified itself enough, but can go on to other than just five-petalled flowers and little brown apples, if we did but know.

So we take the seed as the starting point in this cycle. The woman is the Flesh. She produces all the rest of the flesh, including the intermediary pieces called man – and these curious pieces called man are like stamens that can turn into exquisite-coloured petals. That is, they can beat out the stuff of their life thin, thin, thin, till it is a pink or a purple petal, or a thought, or a Word. And when it is so beaten out that it ceases to be begetting stuff, of the Father, but is spread much wider, expanded and showy: then we say, 'This is the Utmost!' – as everybody will agree that a rose is only a rose because of the petals, and that the rose is the utmost of all that flow of life, called 'Rose'. But what is really 'Rose' is only in that quivering, shimmering flesh of flesh which is the same, unchanged for ever, a constant stream, called if you like rodoplasm, the eternal, the unquestionable, the infinite of the Rose, the Flesh, the Father – which were more properly, the Mother.

So there is the Father – which should be called Mother – then the Son, who is the Utterer, and then the Word. And the Word is that of the Father which, through the Son, is tossed away. It is that part of the Flesh in the Son which is capable of spreading out thin and fine, losing its concentration and completeness, ceasing to be a begetter, and becoming only a vision, a flutter of petals, God rippling through the Son till he breaks in a laugh, called a blossom, that shines and is gone. The vision itself, the flutter of petals, the rose, the Father through the Son wasting himself in a moment of consciousness, consciousness of his own infinitude and gloriousness, a Rose, a Clapping of the Hands, a Spark of Joy thrown off from the Fire to die ruddy in mid-darkness, a Snip of Flame, the Holy Ghost, the Revelation. And so, the eternal Trinity.

And God the Father, the Inscrutable, the Unknowable, we know in the Flesh, in Woman. She is the door for our in-going and our out-coming. In her we go back to the Father: but like the witnesses of the Transfiguration, blind and unconscious.

Yea, like bees in and out of a hive, we come backwards and forwards to our woman. And the Flowers of the World are Words, are Utterance – 'Uttering glad leaves', Whitman said. And we are bees that go between, from the flowers home to the hive and the Queen; for she lies at the centre of the hive, and stands in the way of bees for God the Father, the Almighty, the Unknowable, the Creator. In her all things are born, both words and bees. She is the quick of all the change, the labour, the production.

And the bee, who is a Son, comes home to his Queen as to the Father, in service and humility, for suggestion, and renewal, and identification which is the height of his glory, for begetting. And again the bee goes forth to attend the flowers, the Word in his pride and masterfulness of new strength and new wisdom. And as he comes and goes, so shall man for ever come and go; to his work, his Uttering, wherein he is masterful and proud; come home to his woman, through whom is God the Father, and who is herself, whether she will have it or not, God the Father, before whom the man in his hour is full of reverence, and in whom he is glorified and hath the root of his pride.

But not only does he come and go: it is demanded of him that he come and go. It is the systole and diastole of the Heart, that shall be. The bee comes home to the hive, and the hive expels him to attend the flowers. The hive draws home the bee, the bee leaps off the threshold of the hive, with strength, and is gone. He carries home to the hive his essence, of flowers, his joy in the Word he has uttered, he flies forth again from the hive, carrying to the flowers the strength and vigour of his scrambling body, which is God Almighty in him. So he fetches and carries, carries and fetches.

So the man comes home to woman and to God, so God the Father receives his Son again, a man of the undying flesh; and so the man goes forth from the house of his woman, so God expels him forth to waste himself in utterance, in work, which is only God the Father realizing himself in a moment of forgetfulness.

Thus the eternal working. And it is joy enough to see it, without asking why. For it is as if the Father took delight in seeing himself for a moment unworking, for a moment wasting himself that he might know himself. For every petalled flower, which alone is a Flower, is a work of productiveness. It is a moment of joy, of saying, 'I am I'. And every table or chair a man makes is a self-same waste of his life, a fixing into stiffness and deadness of a moment of himself, for the sake of the glad cry: 'This is I – I am I.' And this glad cry, when we know, is the Holy Ghost, the Comforter.

So, God Eternal, the Father, continues, doing we know not what, not why: we only know He is. And again and again comes the exclamation of joy, or of pain which is joy – like Galileo and Shakespeare and Darwin – which announces 'I am I'.

And in the woman is the eternal continuance, and from the man, in the human race, comes the exclamation of joy and astonishment at new self-revelation, revelation of that which is Woman to a man.

Now every woman, according to her kind, demands that a man shall come home to her with joy and weariness of the work he has done during the day: that he shall then while he is with her, be re-born of her; that in the morning he shall go forth with his new strength.

But if the man does not come home to a woman, leaving her to take account of him, but is a stranger to her; if when he enters her house, he does not become simply her man of flesh, entered into her house as if it were her greater body, to be warmed, and restored, and nourished, from the store the day has given her, then she shall expel him from her house, as a drone. It is as inevitable as the working of the bees, as that a stick shall go down stream.

For in the flesh of the woman does God exact Himself. And out of the flesh of the woman does He demand: 'Carry this of Me forth to utterance.' And if the man deny, or be too weak, then shall the woman find another man, of greater strength. And if, because of the Word, which is the Law, she do not find another man, nor he another woman, then shall they both be destroyed. For he, to get that rest, and warmth, and nourishment which he should have had from her, his woman, must consume his own flesh, and so destroy himself: whether with wine, or other kindling. And she, either her surplus shall wear away her flesh, in sickness, or in lighting up and illuminating old dead Words, or she shall spend it in fighting with her man to make him take her, or she shall turn to her son, and say, 'Be you my Go-between'.

But the man who is the go-between from Woman to Production is the lover of that woman. And if that Woman be his mother, then is he her lover in part only; he carries for her, but is never received into her for his confirmation and renewal, and so wastes himself away in the flesh. The old son-lover was Oedipus. The name of the new one is legion. And if a son-lover take a wife, then is she not his wife, she is only his bed. And his life will be torn in twain, and his wife in her despair shall hope for sons, that she may have her lover in her hour.

## PART TWO

# Early Comment
# and Original Reviews

# 'E. T.' (Jessie Chambers)

## D. H. LAWRENCE:
## A PERSONAL RECORD (1935)

LAWRENCE began to write his autobiographical novel during 1911, which was perhaps the most arid year of his life. He did not tell me himself that he was at work upon this theme. I heard of it through 'Helen'. He had been working on it for the greater part of the year, and it was some time after our brief meeting in October that he sent the entire manuscript to me, and asked me to tell him what I thought of it.

He had written about two-thirds of the story, and seemed to have come to a standstill. The whole thing was somehow tied up. The characters were locked together in a frustrating bondage, and there seemed no way out. The writing oppressed me with a sense of strain. It was extremely tired writing. I was sure that Lawrence had had to force himself to do it. The spontaneity that I had come to regard as the distinguishing feature of his writing was quite lacking. He was telling the story of his mother's married life, but the telling seemed to be at second hand, and lacked the living touch. I could not help feeling that his treatment of the theme was far behind the reality in vividness and dramatic strength. Now and again he seemed to strike a curious, half-apologetic note, bordering on the sentimental. . . . A nonconformist minister whose sermons the mother helped to compose was the foil to the brutal husband. He gave the boy Paul a box of paints, and the mother's heart glowed with pride as she saw her son's budding power. . . . It was story-bookish. The elder brother Ernest, whose short career had always seemed to me most moving and dramatic, was not there at all. I was amazed to find there was no mention of him. The character Lawrence called Miriam was in the story, but placed in a bourgeois setting, in the same family from which he later took the Alvina of *The*

*Lost Girl.* He had placed Miriam in this household as a sort of foundling, and it was there that Paul Morel made her acquaintance.

The theme developed into the mother's opposition to Paul's love for Miriam. In this connection several remarks in this first draft impressed me particularly. Lawrence had written: 'What was it he [Paul Morel] wanted of her [Miriam]? Did he want her to break his mother down in him? Was that what he wanted?'

And again: 'Mrs Morel saw that if Miriam could only win her son's sex sympathy there would be nothing left for her.'

In another place he said: 'Miriam looked upon Paul as a young man tied to his mother's apron-strings.' Finally, referring to the people around Miriam, he said: 'How should they understand her – petty tradespeople!' But the issue was left quite unresolved. Lawrence had carried the situation to the point of deadlock and stopped there.

As I read through the manuscript I had before me all the time the vivid picture of the reality. I felt again the tenseness of the conflict, and the impending spiritual clash. So in my reply I told him I was very surprised that he had kept so far from reality in his story; that I thought what had really happened was much more poignant and interesting than the situations he had invented. In particular I was surprised that he had omitted the story of Ernest, which seemed to me vital enough to be worth telling as it actually happened. Finally I suggested that he should write the whole story again, and keep it true to life.

Two considerations prompted me to make these suggestions. First of all I felt that the theme, if treated adequately, had in it the stuff of a magnificent story. It only wanted setting down, and Lawrence possessed the miraculous power of translating the raw material of life into significant form. That was my first reaction to the problem. My deeper thought was that in the doing of it Lawrence might free himself from his strange obsession with his mother. I thought he might be able to work out the theme in the realm of spiritual reality, where alone it could be worked out, and so resolve the conflict in himself. Since he had elected to deal with the big and difficult subject of his family, and the interactions of the various relationships, I felt he ought to do it faithfully – 'with both hands earnestly', as he was fond of quoting. It seemed to me that if he was able to treat the theme with strict integrity he would thereby walk into freedom, and cast off the trammelling past like an old skin.

The particular issue he might give to the story never entered my head. That was of no consequence. The great thing was that I thought I could see a liberated Lawrence coming out of it. Towards Lawrence's mother I had no bitter feeling, and could have none, because she was his mother. But I felt that he was being strangled in a bond that was even more powerful since her death, and that until he was freed from it he was held in check and unable to develop.

In all this I acted from pure intuition, arising out of my deep knowledge of his situation. I said no word of this to him because I thought it must inevitably work itself out in the novel, provided he treated the subject with integrity. And I had a profound faith in Lawrence's fundamental integrity.

He fell in absolutely with my suggestion and asked me to write what I could remember of our early days, because, as he truthfully said, my recollection of those days was so much clearer than his. I agreed to do so, and began almost at once, but had not got very far when word came that Lawrence was dangerously ill with pneumonia. I was sure he would get better and went on writing the notes for him. When he was convalescent the first thing he wrote was a tiny pencilled message to me, saying: 'Did I frighten you all? I'm sorry. Never mind, I'm soon going to be all right.'

I saw him during the Christmas holiday sitting by the fire in his bedroom, grievously thin, but yet somehow so vital. Whenever I looked at him, I seemed to see the naked flame of life. It was so as he sat in his room on that sunny Saturday morning, from time to time putting a scrap of linen to his lips, and then dropping it into the fire. He looked at me with eyes in which a light would leap, then sink, and leap again. I was staying with 'Helen'. Lawrence asked me where we were going for lunch, and in the way he suddenly turned his head when I told him, I saw the whole bitterness of his illness and his enforced severance from activity.

He asked me if I had written the notes I promised to do, and I told him I had begun to write them before he was ill and just went on. He said he was going to Bournemouth as soon as he was strong enough, and after that he would come and fetch them. This was our first real talk since his mother's funeral. Some of the old magic returned, the sense of inner understanding which was the essence of our friendship. . . .

The writing of the novel (still called 'Paul Morel') now went on apace. Lawrence passed the manuscript on to me as he wrote it, a few sheets at a time, just as he had done with *The White Peacock*, only that this story was written with incomparably greater speed and intensity.

The early pages delighted me. Here was all that spontaneous flow, the seemingly effortless translation of life that filled me with admiration. His descriptions of family life were so vivid, so exact, and so concerned with everyday things we had never even noticed before. There was Mrs Morel ready for ironing, lightly spitting on the iron to test its heat, invested with a reality and significance hitherto unsuspected. It was his power to transmute the common experiences into significance that I always felt to be Lawrence's greatest gift. He did not distinguish between small and great happenings; the common round was full of mystery, awaiting interpretation. Born and bred of working people, he had the rare gift of seeing them from within, and revealing them on their own plane. An incident that particularly pleased me was where Morel was recovering from an accident at the pit, and his friend Jerry came to see him. The conversation of the two men and their tenderness to one another were a revelation to me. I felt that Lawrence was coming into his true kingdom as a creative artist, and an interpreter of the people to whom he belonged. . . . I began to realize that whatever approach Lawrence made to me inevitably involved him in a sense of disloyalty to his mother. Some bond, some understanding, most likely un-formulated and all the stronger for that, seemed to exist between them. It was a bond that definitely excluded me from the only position in which I could be of vital help to him. We were back in the old dilemma, but it was a thousand times more cruel because of the altered circumstances. He seemed to be fixed in the centre of the tension, helpless, waiting for one pull to triumph over the other.

The novel was written in this state of spirit, at a white heat of concentration. The writing of it was fundamentally a terrific fight for a bursting of the tension. The break came in the treatment of Miriam. As the sheets of manuscript came rapidly to me I was bewildered and dismayed at that treatment. I began to perceive that I had set Lawrence a task far beyond his strength. In my confidence I had not doubted that he would work out the problem with integrity. But he burked the real issue. It was his old inability to face his problem squarely. His mother had to be supreme, and for the sake of that supremacy every disloyalty was permissible.

The realization of this slowly dawned on me as I read the manuscript. He asked for my opinion, but comment seemed futile – not merely futile, but impossible. I could not appeal to Lawrence for justice as between his treatment of Mrs Morel and Miriam. He left off coming to see me and sent the manuscript by post. His avoidance of me was significant. I felt it was useless to attempt to argue the matter out with him. Either he was aware of what he was doing and persisted, or he did not know, and in that case no amount of telling would enlighten him. It was one of the things he had to find out for himself. The baffling truth, of course, lay between the two. He was aware, but he was under the spell of the domination that had ruled his life hitherto, and he refused to know. So instead of a release and a deliverance from bondage, the bondage was glorified and made absolute. His mother conquered indeed, but the vanquished one was her son. In *Sons and Lovers* Lawrence handed his mother the laurels of victory.

The Clara of the second half of the story was a clever adaptation of elements from three people, and her creation arose as a complement to Lawrence's mood of failure and defeat. The events related had no foundation in fact, whatever their psychological significance. Having utterly failed to come to grips with his problem in real life, he created the imaginary Clara as a compensation. Even in the novel the compensation is unreal and illusory, for at the end Paul Morel calmly hands her back to her husband, and remains suspended over the abyss of his despair. Many of the incidents struck me as cheap and commonplace, in spite of the hard brilliance of the narration. I realized that I had naïvely credited Lawrence with superhuman powers of detachment.

The shock of *Sons and Lovers* gave the death-blow to our friendship. If I had told Lawrence that I had died before, I certainly died again. I had a strange feeling of separation from the body. The daily life was sheer illusion. The only reality was the betrayal of *Sons and Lovers*. I felt it was a betrayal in an inner sense, for I had always believed that there was a bond between us, if it was no more than the bond of a common suffering. But the brutality of his treatment seemed to deny any bond. That I understood so well what made him do it only deepened my despair. He had to present a distorted picture of our association so that the martyr's halo might sit becomingly on his mother's brow. But to give a recognizable picture of our friendship which yet completely left out the years of devotion to the development of his genius – devotion that had been pure joy – seemed to me like presenting *Hamlet* without the Prince of Denmark. What else but the devotion to a common end had held us together against his mother's repeated assaults? Neither could I feel that he had represented in any degree faithfully the nature and quality of our desperate search for a right relationship. I was hurt beyond all expression. I didn't know how to bear it.

Lawrence had said that he never took sides; but his attitude placed him tacitly on the side of those who had mocked at love – except mother-love. He seemed to have identified himself with the prevailing atmosphere of ridicule and innuendo. It was a fatal alignment, for it made me see him as a philistine of the philistines, and not, as I had always believed, inwardly honouring an unspoken bond, and suffering himself from the strange hostility to love. He had sometimes argued – in an effort to convince himself – that morality and art have nothing to do with one another. However that might be, I could not help feeling that integrity and art have a great deal to do with one another. The best I could think of him was that he had run with the hare and hunted with the hounds. . . . His significance withered and his dimensions shrank. He ceased to matter supremely.

I tried hard to remind myself that after all *Sons and Lovers* was only a novel. It was not the truth, although it must inevitably stand for truth. I could hear in advance Lawrence's protesting voice: 'Of course it isn't the truth. It isn't meant for the truth. It's an adaptation from life, as all art must be. It *isn't* what I think of you; you know it isn't. What shall I put? What do you want me to put . . .?' in a mounting crescendo of irritation and helplessness. I felt that words could only exacerbate the situation. The remedy must be left to time. And as I sat and looked at the subtle distortion of what had been the deepest values of my life, the one gleam of light was the realization that Lawrence had overstated his case; that some day his epic of maternal love and filial devotion would be viewed from another angle, that of his own final despair.

The book was written in about six weeks, under the influence of something amounting almost to frenzy. Although he avoided me Lawrence wanted to know what I thought of the novel. So, after I had studied the last sheets of the manuscript, I suggested that, as I had a holiday on a certain Monday in March, I should spend the week-end with my sister and we might meet and talk about the book. Lawrence replied that he had promised to go on a visit to a schoolmaster friend in Staffordshire on that particular week-end, but he would try to get back in good time on the Sunday. From the tone of his letter I judged that he intended me to have an opportunity of saying anything I wished to say, but it was to be a limited opportunity. I made some notes on minor points and took the manuscript with me. . . .

We went out into the cloudy afternoon and walked past Greasley Church, then took the footpath through the fields where he and my brothers had worked together at hay harvest. Lawrence kept a sharp look-out for violets in the hedgerows.

He said there must be some about because A. [Ada, Lawrence's sister] had seen youths coming home from the pit with bunches of violets and celandines in their hands. At the mention of violets and celandines I had hard work to keep the tears back, because it seemed as if springtime and spring flowers had gone out of my life for ever. Until then his manner had been bleak and forbidding, but now he softened a little and said almost wistfully:

'I thought perhaps you would have something to say about the writing.'

I felt as if I was sinking in deep water. But it was now the eleventh hour, and the time for speaking had gone by, and I merely said:

'I've put some notes in with the manuscript,' and he replied quietly, as though he was suddenly out of breath, 'Oh, all right. I thought you might like to say something. That's all.'

It was not that I would not speak but simply that I could not. Between pride and anguish I found it impossible to tell him that the account he had given of our friendship amounted to a travesty of the real thing. His defensive attitude had kept me at bay, as he intended it should, and now the time was gone. It was too late. I could only remain silent. We spoke no more about the novel and soon turned back towards the cottage. . . .

There was no further attempt at discussion of the novel. Lawrence made no approach to me nor I to him. I returned what few books of his I had, and he replied in a casual note. The more I thought about the situation – and it was impossible to think about anything else – the more certain I became of the futility of attempting to reason the matter out with him. I realized that the entire structure of the story rested upon the attitude he had adopted. To do any kind of justice to our relationship would involve a change in his attitude towards his mother's influence, and of that I was now convinced he was incapable. It was the old situation in a new setting, the necessity for the mother's supremacy. More than a year before he had told me so in exact words, only without referring directly to his mother:

'You are the irremediable thing,' he had said, looking at me as though he would consume me with his eyes. 'You are what *has* to be. You are what cannot be helped. The great thing now is that you should not become bitter.'

It roused my irony that he should take my doom for granted, and in spite of my misery I laughed, and replied:

'No, I don't think I shall turn bitter.' But Lawrence was in such deadly earnest he did not perceive why I laughed. Now, in the novel, he had taken up the same position, and appointed himself judge and executioner. He held over me a doom of negation and futility. It pressed upon me like a weight, making the nights and days a torture. I dreaded lest I should come to fulfil it, as he seemed convinced I must.

# D. H. Lawrence

## LAST WORDS TO MIRIAM (1913)*

Yours is the sullen sorrow,
   The disgrace is also mine;
Your love was intense and thorough,
Mine was the love of a growing flower
   For the sunshine.

You had the power to explore me,
   Blossom me stalk by stalk;
You woke my spirit, and bore me
To consciousness, you gave me the dour
   Awareness – then I suffered a balk.

Body to body I could not
   Love you, although I would.
We kissed, we kissed though we should not.
You yielded, we threw the last cast,
   And it was no good.

You only endured, and it broke
   My craftsman's nerve.
No flesh responded to my stroke;
So I failed to give you the last
   Fine torture you did deserve.

* There are two earlier versions of this poem, one with the same
title, one entitled 'Last Words to Muriel'. See *Collected Poems*, ed.
V. de Sola Pinto and W. Roberts (1964) II 927, 928. G.S.

You are shapely, you are adorned
    But opaque and null in the flesh;
Who, had I but pierced with the thorned
Full anguish, perhaps had been cast
    In a lovely illumined mesh

Like a painted window; the best
    Fire passed through your flesh,
Undrossed it, and left it blest
In clean new awareness. But now
    Who shall take you afresh?

Now who will burn you free
    From your body's deadness and dross?
Since the fire has failed in me,
What man will stoop in your flesh to plough
    The shrieking cross?

A mute, nearly beautiful thing
    Is your face, that fills me with shame
As I see it hardening;
I should have been cruel enough to bring
    You through the flame.

## D. H. Lawrence

## END OF ANOTHER
## HOME HOLIDAY (1913)

When shall I see the half-moon sink again
Behind the black sycamore at the end of the garden?
When will the scent of the dim white phlox
Creep up the wall to me, and in at my open window?

Why is it, the long, slow stroke of the midnight bell
    (Will it never finish the twelve?)
Falls again and again on my heart with a heavy reproach?
The moon-mist is over the village, out of the mist speaks the
    bell,
And all the little roofs of the village bow low, pitiful,
    beseeching, resigned.
– Speak, you my home! what is it I don't do well?

Ah home, suddenly I love you
As I hear the sharp clean trot of a pony down the road,
Succeeding sharp little sounds dropping into silence
Clear upon the long-drawn hoarseness of a train across the
    valley.

      .     .     .

The light has gone out, from under my mother's door:
    That she should love me so! –
    She, so lonely, greying now!
    And I leaving her,
    Bent on my pursuits!

Love is the great Asker.
The sun and the rain do not ask the secret
Of the time when the grain struggles down in the dark.
The moon walks her lonely way without anguish,
Because no one grieves over her departure.

Forever, ever by my shoulder pitiful love will linger,
Crouching as little houses crouch under the mist when I turn.
Forever, out of the mist, the church lifts up a reproachful
    finger,
Pointing my eyes in wretched defiance where love hides her
    face to mourn.

Oh! but the rain creeps down to wet the grain
That struggles alone in the dark,
And asking nothing, patiently steals back again!
The moon sets forth o' nights
To walk the lonely, dusky heights
Serenely, with steps unswerving;
Pursued by no sigh of bereavement,
No tears of love unnerving
Her constant tread:
While ever at my side,
Frail and sad, with grey, bowed head,
The beggar-woman, the yearning-eyed
Inexorable love goes lagging.

The wild young heifer, glancing distraught,
With a strange new knocking of life at her side
    Runs seeking a loneliness.
The little grain draws down the earth, to hide.
Nay, even the slumberous egg, as it labours under the
    shell
    Patiently to divide and self-divide,
Asks to be hidden, and wishes nothing to tell.

But when I draw the scanty cloak of silence over my eyes
Piteous love comes peering under the hood;
Touches the clasp with trembling fingers, and tries
To put her ears to the painful sob of my blood;
While her tears soak through to my breast,
     Where they burn and cauterise.


        ·    ·    ·


    The moon lies back and reddens.
    In the valley a corncrake calls
      Monotonously,
    With a plaintive, unalterable voice, that deadens
      My confident activity;
    With a hoarse, insistent request that falls
      Unweariedly, unweariedly,
      Asking something more of me,
        Yet more of me.

# Reviews from

## Athenaeum

MR LAWRENCE'S new novel is a fine, but not altogether a well-made piece of work. A certain distortion arises from the fact that, while all the other characters are drawn, as it were, in the third person, the hero is drawn in the first. The pronoun 'I' is not, indeed, employed for him, but the author has lived so completely within his creation that the narrative reads like an autobiography – and, as discerning readers know, autobiographies are less likely than biographies to produce a lifelike portrait. We are not, at the end of the story, left understanding the nature of the man about whom it is told. No doubt he himself would not, in real life, have understood it; but we cannot help thinking that to complete his achievement the novelist should have made the reader do so.

Nor is the young woman who is the first – and perhaps the last – love of the hero satisfactorily realized. Many men, and perhaps most women, will say to themselves as they read: 'Yes, this is how Miriam seemed to Paul, but this is not what Miriam was.' We suspect – and it is a tribute to the strength of the illusion created – that, if the girl's story had been written, we should have found her by no means so abnormal a person as represented, and her wayward lover considerably more comprehensible.

But, although we may rebel, we are held captive from the first page to the last, and certain figures will, we think, remain engraved upon the memory. The story is a 'family piece', and all are, with one exception, vividly drawn. The sister's figure is hardly represented at all, and an impression is thus tacitly conveyed that the one girl did not count in the family, and that the mother, whose relation to her sons forms the very kernel of the book, ignored her daughter. Yet the rare glimpses allowed of this daughter indicate a strong and interesting personality, and in real life she would probably have loomed large on the horizon of her slightly younger brother. In the book, she is nothing to him; the two influences in his life are his mother and the girl who understands his artistic work and who craves, as he does, for fuller education. Of these two it is not his contemporary whom he really loves and understands; his mother is far closer to him; she clings to him jealously, fighting against the younger woman's power, and succeeding in holding the pair apart. With his mother's death the son's life loses value and coherence; he is left, indeed, derelict. Her character is a real triumph.

Brilliant, too, is the figure of the hopelessly shallow girl who captured the first-born of the household; and pathetically true is his perception of her nature and his own bondage.

(21 June 1913)

## Saturday Review

WHEN were there written novels so strange as these of Mr Lawrence? Now that he has given us three of them we should be able to make some estimate of his position among writers, yet there is about him something wilful which eludes judgment. Passages in *Sons and Lovers* tempt us to place him in a high class; and it is indeed a good book, even though it has pages where the author's vision is revealed only behind a dense cloud. As a story it is the record of the lives of a miner and his family in the middle counties of England, and from *The White Peacock* we knew how well the Derbyshire and Nottinghamshire country would be pictured. It can now be added that the scenes from the towns are little less good. The ruling idea in the book is the pitiful wastage of the best in men and women, and it is first shown in the persons of Morel and his wife. The former is physically a grand specimen of a race which puts its strength into manual labour, but he is ruined by drink, for his will is always weak. Mrs Morel is a good housewife and a decent woman. Her superior ways mark her to her husband as a lady; yet she shirks none of the duties which his mate should perform for him, the children, and the home. Unhappily there is in her something of the shrew, and the association between the pair serves only to bring out their unpleasant sides. The young family grows up zealous for the mother; but with the touch of skill Mr Lawrence can show the father as the good fellow whom these others never knew. 'He', we read, 'always sang when he mended boots because of the jolly sound of hammering'; and in that single sentence is revealed the human creature who should have had pure joy of life and an author whose inspiration leaves behind the common artifices of the novelist. There are many other places where the writer quite surprises us by his power to make the narrative pass from fiction into glowing reality, and as an example we cannot do better than quote from the scene where young Paul and his sweetheart are climbing in the ruined tower: 'They continued to mount the winding staircase. A high wind, blowing through the loopholes, went rushing up the shaft and filled the girl's skirts like a balloon, so that she was ashamed, until he took the hem of her dress and held it down for her. He did it perfectly simply, as he would have picked up her glove.' No man could have invented this piece of description at the factory of the desk; it is a fragment of life, though we cannot know whether it belongs to the world of fact or had its genesis in some glorious flash of imagination. Origin, however, matters nothing. The passage remains as one which not a novelist in a hundred could produce.

Paul Morel, the miner's second son, is the chief person in the book, and his tragedy is his devotion to his mother, for she absorbs almost everything in him but his passions. Miriam, the girl of the tower episode, does battle for him. Despite her fierce purity she gives herself to his desire, but she cannot hold him even by her sacrifice, and he drifts into a passionate friendship with a second woman. The idea of waste still rules the story. The mother, who has dreaded the influence of Miriam on his affections, almost welcomes the intrigue with Clara, because the latter is less exacting in her demands. Puritan as she is, Mrs Morel condones the affair with a married woman in order to keep the

greater part of her son for herself. The strife between the generations is admirably suggested, and we know of no active English
novelist – today – who has Mr Lawrence's power to put in
words the rise and fall of passion. The death of the mother and
Paul's derelict state are the ends to which the story naturally
leads, for the author is too good an artist to allow a conclusion
which could stultify the force of all that he has built on the
characters of his people. What is wrong in the book is the fre-
quent intrusion of the writer. The men and women use words
which are his and not their own; their reading is in the literature
for which he cares; often they express thoughts which belong to
him and not to them. Mr Lawrence's inability to efface himself is
now his most serious weakness, for the faulty construction of his
earlier work is in no way evident in *Sons and Lovers*. After
reading most of the more 'important' novels of the present year,
we can say that we have seen none to excel it in interest and
power; the sum of its defects is astonishingly large, but we only
note it when they are weighed against the sum of its own
qualities.                                                      (21 June 1913)

# *Bookman*

THERE is occasionally a fitness in the association of a particular
publisher with a particular book and that of Messrs Duckworth
& Co. with *Sons and Lovers*, Mr D. H. Lawrence's latest novel,
is an example of it. The book has naturally a place in a list which
includes such authors as John Galsworthy, Cunninghame
Graham and Charles Doughty, to name only three of the many
who have enriched the literature of today with work which is, in
some sense, esoteric, claiming acknowledgment and understanding from a limited circle of readers rather than from that
general public for whose accommodation the circulating libraries
have their being. It has nothing of urbanity and no trace of the
humorous and faintly contemptuous patronage which is common

– and probably rather difficult to avoid – in novels dealing with a particular piece of country and class of people. Its descriptions and interpretations are convincing as experience is convincing; Mr Lawrence is on his own ground and presents it with an assured intimacy of knowledge that never fails or blurs. It is Derbyshire and Nottingham of which he writes, the Derbyshire in which the grime of coal-mines is close neighbour to open country of singular charm, and the quality of it is in the very texture of his story.

The sons and lovers of the title-page are the sons of Gertrude Morel, who married a miner and lived in the Bottoms at Bestwood. Mr Lawrence wastes sympathy on none of his characters; it is much if he gives them an approving word; but Mrs Morel is drawn at fullest length, as faithfully as if he loved her. Her husband, a fine and florid animal at the time of her marriage, is shallow and futile, a creature of easy appetites easily slaked; the book comes upon her at a time when she has to suffice for herself in all that side of her life which is responsible and not merely material. She was clear headed, faithful to her ideas of right, full of strength and purpose, and with it she did not lack her spice of shrewishness.

It was with her children that she was successful, and chiefly so with her second son, Paul, the most notable and by far the most complex and ineffectual lover of them all. He shares with his mother the centre of Mr Lawrence's stage; for him her harsh righteousness tones itself to a softer key. With his diffidence and fastidiousness there goes a strain of the artist; he has the makings of a painter in him; he concludes by being extraordinarily ineffectual both as a lover and a man; but it is the author's gift to show him as not the less real for that. It is impossible to summarise the tale of his emotional adventures; there is hardly anything in the book that can be conveyed at all in synopsis, the whole of it develops itself so truly that there is scarcely an episode which would not lose significance if it were detached from its context.

It is a novel of outstanding quality, singular in many respects and in none more so than in the author's constancy to his artistic purpose, which never suffers him to see his people in a dramatic or spectacular light or on a level higher or lower than his own. The fact that they exist suffices him without calling them names, whether good or bad, his business is to show them, dispassionately and accurately. He writes with a nervous pliancy which is a joy to read.                                          (P.G., August 1913)

## Nation

IT is hard to see why the author chose the coal fields of Derbyshire as his setting, and for his hero the son of a miner, unless, indeed, he wished to imply that the free thinking and free living of a certain fashionable London society have penetrated, like the tango and the victrola, to the lower classes. The story will leave a gloomy impression on most readers. It is too strongly grasped and wrought out to be negligible, and will force many, in spite of themselves, to accept it as a true picture. As to the general background, there can be no question that the writer has his eye on the object. Life in the Morel household, hard as it is, is no more severe than an occasional miner's wife has to contend with. Mrs Morel is obliged not only to wring enough from her hard-drinking husband to make both ends meet, but to bear him children in rapid succession; and the early chapters also relate her struggle to maintain the ideals to which before marriage she has been accustomed. In this battle lies the book's real charm and pathos. The mother's relation to her children, especially two sons, is described with the firm knowledge that brings conviction.

The second son, Paul Morel, is the central character of the story. Having learned to paint, though he continues in a clerkship throughout the book, he is promptly endowed by the author with all the heartache expected of great genius. He loves Miriam, the attractive daughter of a farmer, yet cannot marry her because she is too shadowy. Instead, he claims her body, and, passion having cooled, is convinced that his soul requires pastures new.

He has a similar and more extended relation with a young married woman living apart from her husband, and again interprets the vicissitudes of physical desire in spiritual terms. At length his mother dies, after long-drawn-out suffering with cancer; rather, her actual end is accomplished by him by means of an overdose of morphia, intended, one must believe, not only to relieve her anguish, but his own as well. Then nothing is left for him. Miriam offers to marry him, but he refuses, and walks forth into the night.

Paul's 'affairs' are the indulgence of an egotist, whose egotism has no large transforming power.          (vol. XCVII, no. 2528)

# New Republic

MR D. H. LAWRENCE finds himself in agreement with other writers in one important respect. He, too, like the vast majority of fictionists of all time, looks upon the successful mating of his characters as the fundamental problem of his story. And however much we may sometimes tire of the conventional 'and they lived happily ever after', we must admit that novelists are right in focusing attention upon this point. Whether for good or evil, almost every mature fantasy about life probably has an erotic core, so that we are hardly capable of thinking it through without including a marriage idyll by means of which we unconsciously strive to recall that secure haven of love which we dimly associate with our childhood. The melodramatic novelist naïvely looks upon all obstacles to mating as coming entirely from without. More mature writers realize subtler difficulties and put their emphasis almost entirely upon the inner conflicts, but they usually manage to end with a successful mating.

That is just what Mr Lawrence never really succeeds in doing. With him the inner conflicts, instead of being gradually resolved, luxuriate to inordinate proportions until in the end they prove too much both for the author and his characters. Not that all mating is excluded from his pages. But when marriage does finally overtake some of his characters it usually comes as a kind of dismissal from our attention, or with just that novelistic conventionality to which readers rightly object. The whole creative warmth of the author is automatically withdrawn, and these superficially successful matings, so evidently punished by Mr Lawrence's neglect, inevitably leave us cold. To the matings which he has most at heart he invariably opposes insuperable obstacles.

Both *The Trespasser* and *The White Peacock* are early studies in mis-mating. These novels already foreshadow the born stylist and reveal Mr Lawrence as a writer of puzzling importance. But the mis-matings they portray remain obscurely motivated and therefore seem arbitrary; the psychological justification is often inadequate or obscure. We do not understand them, and hesitate to accept them. The same criticism applies to Mr Lawrence's play, *The Widowing of Mrs Holroyd*. We see that Mrs Holroyd hates her husband, but we do not see so clearly why her love for him has died, drunkard though he is. For the author, in spite of himself, has made him lovable notwithstanding his vices, so that his death comes as a sorrow and a rebuke to his wife. The play is more powerful than the novels if only because a livid hate expressed on the stage by an impassioned woman carries its own conviction.

*Sons and Lovers* marks an astonishing change in its author. If this slow-moving, profound, almost too inevitable study leaves the fascinated reader disturbed and exhausted, it is surely no less exhaustive of the author's true inwardness. Here Mr Lawrence has found the very core of himself; here he has dipped deep into his own childhood, setting down all that he ever knew or felt. We notice a sudden exquisite refinement of psychological texture, a new, painstaking reverence for the most subtle and intangible details of motivation. The problem of mis-mating is no longer studied in an already established marital relation; here it is not a matter of mis-mating at all but of a radical inability to mate. This inability Mr Lawrence seeks to explain entirely in terms of his hero's emotional relation to his parents.

That is the really new and contributive thing about *Sons and Lovers*. Paul Morel's childhood unfolds in the vitiated atmosphere of an already unhappy marriage. In the married life of the Morels Mr Lawrence for the first time gives us a mis-mating which both he and we thoroughly understand. The marriage of this drunken, bullying, morally weak-fibred miner to a woman of superior breeding and a stern, sensitive, puritanically unsensuous temperament, was foredoomed to failure. Her hatred and aversion for him is absorbed by her child almost from the cradle, so that at the age of six Paul prays that his father may be killed. Cut off from companionship with his father – and there can be no doubt that a child learns to love the father largely through imitating its mother – Paul abnormally concentrates all his affection upon one parent.

Under the strain of these relations the boy develops a premature emotional maturity. His childish heart is torn between anguish for his abused mother and a scarcely repressed hatred for his brutal father. Mrs Morel, her affection for her husband completely atrophied, now turns altogether to her son and deliberately courts his allegiance. He becomes her confidant and her consoler, a quiet, wordly-wise child whose natural initiative is gradually deadened by the burden of this unequal responsibility, while at the same time the too great absorption in his mother effeminizes him. At a time when most children already display the first poetic tentatives of the mating impulse in ideal comradeships with playmates of the opposite sex, Paul dreams only of running away with his mother and living alone with her for the rest of his life.

By the time Paul reaches adolescence the distortion is already complete. He finds himself attracted to Miriam Leivers, a shy, beautiful girl who idealizes him. But the prospect of marrying her fills him only with unhappiness and a strange, paralyzing sense of death. The author now boldly underlines the mutual infatuation of mother and son. A jealous conflict, in which Paul is the helpless pawn, ensues between the two women. Paul gradually becomes persuaded of the unreality of his and Miriam's feelings, and returns to his exultant mother with the tragic conviction that while she is alive no other woman can have place in his affections.

There is a final flaring up of his mating impulse towards Clara Dawes, a married woman of strong, sensuous appeal. While under her influence he returns to Miriam and finally possesses both women, hovering for a time between what are for him the sacred and profane loves of his life. His consciousness that with Clara he is merely indulging in a temporary liaison with a married woman makes it easier for him to give himself to her. But in the end Mrs Morel triumphs again and brings Paul to her death-bed, a confessed and repentant lover. Her death, now desired and even criminally hastened by him as an emancipation from an intolerable situation, makes her triumph only the more complete and leaves Paul standing before us a helpless, tragic, pathetically childish figure. In a final unforgettable chapter Mr Lawrence pictures him as a human derelict set adrift, with the great nostalgia for death in his heart, and living merely in the memory of a relation which, hallowed only in childhood, has grown utterly ruinous in its perpetuations.

No summary can convey the pathos of *Sons and Lovers*. With all its power and its passion, it remains to a certain extent incomprehensible. We may, for the moment, accept it intuitively. But we hesitate to accept it in its implications. The very idea that an excess of mother love should prove so disastrous to an individual's fate seems monstrous. Instinctively we look upon this as an exceptional case, and fortify ourselves against it by calling the book morbid or perverse. Mr Lawrence himself has not come to our aid with any supplementary theory, nor, fortunately, does he weaken the natural eloquence of his artistry by any attempt to generalize.

How deeply felt, how little reasoned, the reaction has been with him may be gathered from a reading of his *Love Poems*. These astonishingly self-revealing lyrics repeat, with almost monotonous regularity, Paul's most intimate psychic conflicts. And it would not be at all difficult, going back now, to show that the earlier novels and the play are also, in their essence, nothing more than unclarified and fragmentary expressions of the same personal experience before Mr Lawrence had arrived at the searching and pitiless insight which in *Sons and Lovers* makes him such a memorable artist. Hatred of the father and too much love of the mother are the *leitmotifs* of everything this author has written.

In order to understand Mr Lawrence fully we must go beyond his works. Fiction is at best a specialized and limited way of conveying the truth. A novel based upon the truth of the evolutionary theory, poetically visioned by the author at a time when that theory was not yet a part of general knowledge, would, despite all artistic merit, leave a certain margin of incredulity until, let us say, Huxley's lectures had made evolution a household term. In precisely the same way our completer understanding of *Sons and Lovers* depends upon our knowledge of a theory. For without the Freudian psycho-sexual theories *Sons and Lovers* remains an enigma; with it we see that artist and scientist supplement each other, that each in his own way attests to the same truth.

The methods necessarily differ. Where Mr Lawrence particularizes so passionately Freud generalizes. Freud has proved beyond cavil that the parental influence regularly determines the mating impulse. The child's attachment to the parent of opposite sex becomes the prototype of all later love relations. The feeling is so strong and even fraught with such intense jealousy of the parent of the same sex, that all children seem to entertain conscious and unconscious fantasies in which the rival parent is either killed or removed. In the normal development this first infatuation is gradually obliterated from memory by widening associations and by transference, but the unconscious impress remains, so that every man tends to choose for his mate a woman who has associative connections for him with the early infantile image of his mother, while the woman also makes her choice in relation to her father. As soon as there is any disturbance of the balanced influence of both parents upon the child there follows an abnormal concentration upon the beloved parent. To such distortion of the normal erotic development Freud attaches the greatest importance, seeing in it the major cause of all neurotic disturbances.

Of this *Sons and Lovers* is an eloquent example. A distortion so great that it precludes all mating is not only prejudicial to the individual's true happiness but may lead to an atrophy of all initiative. Paul constantly associates the feeling of death with his inability to mate, and that too is psychologically sound. We recognize the Paul in us. For though we may dislike a happy ending in our novel, we cannot but prefer it in our lives.

(Alfred Kuttner, 10 April 1915)

# PART THREE

# Recent Criticism

*Alfred Booth Kuttner*

# A FREUDIAN APPRECIATION (1916)

I

POETS and novelists often strive for impressiveness in their creations by dealing in strange plots and adventures or in monstrous and unnatural loves. The advantages gained may well be called in question: to be grotesque is hardly ever to be great and the bizarre may survive as a demerit after it is exhausted as a sensation. The great literature of life is after all built around the commonplace. The *Odyssey* treats of a bad case of homesickness, a thing which we all understand perfectly. The drama of Oedipus depicts an incestuous relationship, and we do not have to be told that it is horrible. What distinguishes enduring literature is not novelty, but freshness of feeling, and that pointed insight into life which reveals a vivid personality keenly alive. *Sons and Lovers* has the great distinction of being very solidly based upon a veritable commonplace of our emotional life; it deals with a son who loved his mother too dearly, and with a mother who lavished all her affection upon her son.

Neither this distinction nor its undeniable freshness and often amazing style would of itself entitle Mr D. H. Lawrence's novel to anything beyond an appreciative book review. But it sometimes happens that a piece of literature acquires an added significance by virtue of the support it gives to the scientific study of human motives. Literary records have the advantage of being the fixed and classic expression of human emotions which in the living individual are usually too fluid and elusive for deliberate study. The average man, subjected to what seems to him a kind of psychological vivisection, is apt to grow reticent, and mankind must often be convicted through its literature of impulses which under direct scrutiny it would acknowledge only with the greatest reluctance or else deny altogether. Literature thus becomes an invaluable accessory to the psychologist, who usually does well to regard with suspicion any new generalization from his researches for which the whole range of literary expression yields no corroboration. But if he can succeed in finding support there his position is immensely strengthened. For a new truth about ourselves, which may seem altogether grotesque and impossible when presented to us as an arid theory, often gains unexpected confirmation when presented to us in a powerful work of literature as an authentic piece of life. When at last we recognize ourselves we like the thrill of having made a discovery.

*Sons and Lovers* possesses this double quality to a high degree. It ranks high, very high as a piece of literature and at the same time it embodies a theory which it illustrates and exemplifies with a completeness that is nothing less than astonishing. Fortunately there can be no doubt as to the authenticity of the author's inspiration. For it would be fatal if the novel had been written with the express purpose of illustrating a theory: it would, by that very admission, be worthless as a proof of that theory. But it happens that Mr Lawrence has already produced notable work, mainly some early and evidently autobiographical poems, which show his preoccupation with the identical theme. *Sons and Lovers* is thus truly creative, in that it is built up internally – as any masterpiece must be – out of the psychic conflicts of the author, and any testimony which it may bear to the truth of the theory involved will therefore be first hand.

The theory to which I have been referring is Professor Sigmund Freud's theory of the psychological evolution of the emotion of love as finally expressed by a man or a woman towards a member of the other sex, and the problem which Mr Lawrence voices is the struggle of a man to emancipate himself from his maternal allegiance and to transfer his affections to a woman who stands outside of his family circle. What the poet has seen as a personal problem the scientist has formulated as a theory. I shall outline the problem first and then relate it to the theory. If the theory can succeed in generalizing the truth which Mr Lawrence's novel presents the reader will realize with fresh force that fiction, to be great art, must be based upon human verities.

## II

First we shall see how it happened that the mother in this story came to lavish all her affections upon her son. In the opening chapter Mrs Morel, the wife of a Derbyshire coal-miner, is expecting her third child, the boy Paul, who is to become the central figure of the story. Her life with her husband has already turned out to be a complete fiasco. He is a drunkard and a bully, a man with whom she shares neither intellectual, moral nor religious sympathies. What strikes her most about Morel is that he presents a striking contrast to her father, who was to her 'the type of all men'. For he had been a harsh, puritan type, given to theology and ignoring 'all sensuous pleasure', while Morel is the very opposite; warm, sensuous and indulgent, with a 'rich ringing laugh' and a 'red, moist mouth'. It is this sensuous quality in Morel which overwhelms and confounds her; she goes down before the sheer, impersonal male in him. After the sex illusion has worn off somewhat Mrs Morel makes an attempt to draw nearer to her husband. But the clash of personalities is stronger than the transitory tie of their poetized passion and Morel's habitual drunkenness, his indulgent and shiftless ways, and his temperamental dishonesty are mercilessly flayed by his almost fanatically moral and religious wife. It is very easy for her to loathe him. At the time of the birth of her third child the breach is already irreparable. Mrs Morel dreads the coming of another child, conceived unwillingly out of a loveless relation, and at the sight of it a sense of guilt steals over her. She will atone: 'With all her force, with all her soul she would make up to it for having brought it into the world unloved. She would love it all the more now it was hers; carry it in her love.' Towards Paul she feels, as to none of the other children, that she must make up to him for an injury or a sin committed by her and that he must recompense her for all that she has missed in her shattered love for her husband.

All the early formative influences in Paul's life radiate from his mother. Physically he is more delicate than the other children so that his illnesses tend to further her concentration upon him still more. Paul is a 'pale, quiet child' who seems 'old for his years' and 'very conscious of what other people felt, particularly his mother. When she fretted he understood, and could have no peace. His soul seemed always attentive to her.' His mother and for a time his sister Annie are his only real companions. His brother William is too old to be his playmate and other children play no rôle in his early childhood. One vicious bond of sympathy unites all the Morel children; their common hate and contempt for their father. This feeling poisons the whole family life. Often, of a windy night in their creaking house, the children lie awake listening in terror for his drunken return, his banging fists and the muffled voice of their mother. The strain is greatest upon Paul. Towards evening he grows restless and stays near his mother, waiting for his father's coming and the usual scene of abuse and violence. Already at an early age these hostile feelings take definite shape. He often prays: 'Lord, let my father die.' And then, with a kind of guilty conscience: 'Let him not be killed at pit.' One incident in particular stands out in his memory. Morel has just blackened his wife's eyes and William, then already a tall and muscular youth, threatens to beat him. Paul aches to have him do it; it is his own wish which he cannot carry out. Later, when he is older, he almost does it himself, but for his mother's fainting, and his physical encounters with other men are tinged with a deadly animosity, as if the memory of that earlier hate had lingered on in him. We must remember that Paul had been born into an atmosphere of parental violence; when still a baby his father hurled a drawer at his mother so that the blood had trickled down upon the child's head. Indelible among his earliest impressions must have been that gross and terrifying figure, threatening his life and that of his mother, whose convulsive movements to protect him must have aroused an answering quiver in the child.

The early relations between mother and child are full of a delicate and poetic charm. Paul's admiration for his mother knows no bounds; her presence is always absorbing. Often, at the sight of her, 'his heart contracts with love'. Everything he does is for her, the flowers he picks as well as the prizes he wins at school. His mother is his intimate and his confidante, he has no other chums. When Morel is confined to the hospital through an accident in the mine, Paul joyfully plays the husband: 'I'm the man in the house now.' He is happiest when alone with her. By this time the interaction between mother and son is complete; she lives in him and he in her. In fact his whole attitude towards her is but the answer which she gradually evokes from him as her whole life finds expression in her son. 'In the end she shared everything with him without knowing. . . . She waited for his coming home in the evening, and then she unburdened herself of all she had pondered, or of all that had occurred to her during the day. He sat and listened with his earnestness. The two shared lives.' The emotional correspondence between them is striking, 'his heart contracted with pain of love of her' just as from the very beginning she has always 'felt a mixture of anguish in her love for him'. Mother and son are one; the husband is completely effaced and the father exists merely as a rival.

But now Paul is to strike out for himself. He takes up an occupation and finds himself attracted to women. His mother's whole emphasis has always been towards making Paul interested in some other occupation than his father's dirty digging, as a protest against the sordidness of the life that she herself has been compelled to lead with him. She therefore encourages the boy's liking for pretty things, for flowers and sunsets and fancy stuffs, and is delighted when his slender artistic endowment begins to express itself in pencil and paint. Her emotional revolt against her husband here takes an esthetic turn, as people are often driven to beauty by their loathing of the ugly, and it is interesting to note that Mrs Morel's tendencies to estheticize Paul and to effeminate him go hand in hand, as if the two sprang from a common root. Paul never becomes a real artist. He uses his painting to please his mother and to court his women, but in the crises of his life his art means nothing to him either as a consolation or as a satisfying expression. As his painting is essentially dilettante and unre-munerative, his mother apprentices him in a shop for surgical appliances where the process of effeminization goes on through his contact with the girls and women with whom he works. He himself has no ambition. All that he wants is 'quietly to earn his thirty or thirty-five shillings a week somewhere near home, and then, when his father died, have a cottage with his mother, paint and go out as he liked, and live happy ever after'. Not, like any normal boy, to strike out for himself, to adventure, to emulate and surpass his father, but to go on living with his mother forever! That is the real seed of Paul's undoing. We shall now trace the various attempts on his part to emancipate himself from his mother by centering his affections upon some other woman.

The first woman to attract Paul is Miriam Leivers, a shy, exalted and romantic girl who leads a rather lonely life with her parents and brothers on a neighbouring farm. Paul's approach is characteristically indirect; he begins by avoiding the girl and cultivating her mother. Meanwhile Miriam, piqued by the neglect of this well-mannered boy, who seems so gentle and superior, has fallen in love with him. Paul is fascinated but uneasy and fights shy of personal intimacy with her. The intensity of her emotions frightens him and impresses him as unwholesome. He finds her growing absorption in him strangely discomfiting: 'Always something in his breast shrank from these close, intimate, dazzled looks of hers.' His feminine attitude towards her tends to reverse the usual method of courtship; it is Miriam who has to seek him out, to call for him, and make sure of his coming again. Paul tries to approach her in two ways; through his art and as her teacher. Both methods are really self-defensive, they are barriers that he erects against Miriam to prevent anything too personal from arising between them, to keep his real self, as it were, inviolate. For as a painter he distracts her attention from himself to his work and as her instructor he wields an authority with which he can keep her emotions in check by overawing her. Something about her is always putting him on edge, he loses his temper at her very easily and feels a dawning impulse of cruelty. 'It made his blood rouse to see her there, as it were, at his mercy.' Sometimes he feels an actual hatred for her. And immediately he thinks of his mother: 'He was thankful in his heart and soul that he had his mother, so sane and wholesome.'

Paul resists every intimation that he is falling in love with Miriam. He indignantly repudiates his mother's insinuation that he is courting and hastens to assure Miriam: 'We aren't lovers, we are friends.' And Miriam, who has already gone so far, tries to fortify herself with a prayer. 'O Lord, let me not love Paul Morel. Keep me from loving him, if I ought not to love him.' But her love breaks through again and her healthier instincts triumph. Henceforth Paul can do with her as he will. But he can do nothing with her love because he cannot return it. Love seems to him like a 'very terrible thing'. The honest and more impersonal passion that he feels for her frightens him. 'He was afraid of her. The fact that he might want her as a man wants a woman had in him been suppressed into a shame.' He cannot even kiss her. And he hates her again because she makes him despise himself. They gradually move to the edge of a quarrel.

And now Mrs Morel makes her appeal. Almost from the first she has mistrusted Miriam. She fears that Miriam will absorb him and take him away from her. 'She is one of those who will want to suck a man's soul out till he has none of his own left.' Her jealousy revels in the exaggerated simile of the vampire. 'She exults – she exults as she carries him off from me. . . . She's not like an ordinary woman . . . she wants to absorb him . . . she will suck him up.' So she throws down the gauntlet to her rival. She makes Paul feel wretched, as only a mother can make a son feel, whenever he has been with Miriam. Her comments grow spiteful and satiric; she no longer takes the trouble to hide her jealousy and plagues him like a cast woman. 'Is there nobody else to talk to? . . . Yes, I know it well – I am old. And therefore I may stand aside; I have nothing more to do with you. You only want me to wait on you – the rest is for Miriam.' It sounds like a wife's bitter reproach to her husband. Paul writhes under her words and hates Miriam for it. But Mrs Morel does not stop there. She makes the final, ruthless, cowardly appeal.

'And I've never – you know, Paul – I've never had a husband – not – really –'

He stroked his mother's hair, and his mouth was on her throat.

'Well, I don't love her, mother,' he murmured, bowing his

head and hiding his eyes on her shoulder in misery. His mother kissed him, a long, fervent kiss.

'My boy!' she said, in a voice trembling with passionate love. Without knowing, he gently stroked her face. (ch. VIII)

Thus she wins him back. He will continue to console her for her husband. There follows the scene where Paul almost thrashes his drunken father and implores his mother not to share the same bed with him. It is a crisis in his life: '. . . he was at peace because he still loved his mother best. It was the bitter peace of resignation.'

But there is some resistance in him still. For a time he stands divided between his two loves. 'And he felt dreary and hopeless between the two.' In church, sitting between them, he feels at peace: 'uniting his two loves under the spell of the place of worship'. But most of the time he is torn between the two women. He does not understand his feelings. 'And why did he hate Miriam and feel so cruel towards her at the thought of his mother?' His emotions towards Miriam are constantly changing. Sometimes his passion tries to break through. But it cannot free itself. 'I'm so damned spiritual with *you* always!' He blames her for the humiliating sense of impotence which he feels. It is all her fault. He transfers all his inhibitions to her and consciously echoes his mother's accusations. 'You absorb, absorb, as if you must fill yourself up with love, because you've got a shortage somewhere.' When her love for him flames out to confound him he takes refuge by talking about his work. There at least some freedom is left for them both. 'All his passion, all his wild blood, went into this intercourse with her, when he talked and conceived his work.' But at last he tells her that he does not love her, that he cannot love her physically. 'I can only give friendship – it's all I'm capable of – it's a flaw in my make-up. . . . Let us have done.' And finally he writes: 'In all our relations no body enters. I do not talk to you through the senses – rather through the spirit. That is why we cannot love in common sense. Ours is not an everyday affection.' Thus he tries to spiritualize their relations out of existence. He would persuade himself of his own impotence.

Paul's whole experience with Miriam has thrown him back

upon his mother; he gets away from Miriam by returning to her. 'He had come back to his mother. Hers was the strongest tie in his life. When he thought round, Miriam shrank away. There was a vague, unreal feeling about her. . . . And in his soul was a feeling of the satisfaction of self-sacrifice because he was faithful to her [his mother]. She loved him first, he loved her first' (ch. IX). He is her child again and for a time he feels content. They go off on a charming excursion to Lincoln Cathedral. He behaves like a lover out with his girl, buying her flowers and treating her. Suddenly there surges up in him a childhood memory of the time when his mother was young and fair, before life wrung her dry and withered her. If only he had been her eldest son so that his memory of her could be still more youthful! 'What are you old for!' he said, mad with his own impotence. 'Why can't you walk, why can't you come with me to places?' He does not like to have such an old sweetheart.

At the same time his whole outlook upon life also grows childish again. When his sister Annie marries he tries to console his mother. 'But I shan't marry, mother. I shall live with you, and we'll have a servant.' She doubts him and he proceeds to figure it out. 'I'll give you till seventy-five. There you are, I'm fat and forty-four. Then I'll marry a staid body. See! . . . And we'll have a pretty house, you and me, and a servant, and it'll be just all right.' His plans for the future have not changed. He thinks at twenty-two as he thought at fourteen, like a child that goes on living a fairy-tale. But it is a false contentment and he pays the penalty for it. In resigning the natural impulse to love he also resigns the impulse to live. Life cannot expand in him, it is turned back upon itself and becomes the impulse to die. Paul makes the great refusal. 'What is happiness!' he cried. 'It's nothing to me! How *am* I to be happy? . . . He had that poignant carelessness about himself, his own suffering, his own life, which is a form of slow suicide.' Mrs Morel sees the danger and divines the remedy. 'At this rate she knew he would not live. . . . She wished she knew some nice woman – she did not know what she wished, but left it vague.' But now she knows that she can no longer hold her son to her exclusively.

At this point Paul begins to turn to another woman, Clara
Dawes, a friend of Miriam. She is married, but lives separated
from her husband. Paul has known her for some time before
becoming intimate with her. She exerts a frankly sensual attraction upon him without having any of that mystical unattainable-
ness about her which he felt so strongly with Miriam. Her
presence has had the effect of gradually seducing him away from
Miriam without his knowing it. There would be less difficulty
with her. She is a married woman and is unhappy with her husband, like his mother. To love her would not be so momentous a
thing, he would be less unfaithful to his mother if he had an
affair with a woman who already belonged to someone else.
Their relations threaten to become typical of the young man and
the woman of thirty. 'She was to him extraordinarily provocative, because of the knowledge she seemed to possess, and
gathered fruit of experience . . .' The question of marriage would
hardly enter; he could go on loving his mother. But still he is
inhibited. 'Sex had become so complicated in him that he would
have denied that he ever could want Clara or Miriam or any
woman whom he *knew*. Sex desire was a sort of detached thing,
that did not belong to a woman.' Clara's first service to him is to
talk to him like a woman of the world and thus correct his self-
delusion about Miriam: '. . . she doesn't want any of your soul
communion. That's your own imagination. She wants you.' He
objects. ' "You've never tried," she answered' (ch. x). Thus she
gives him courage to do what he never could have done of his
own accord.

The force which drives him back to Miriam is nothing but
the sheer, pent-up sexual desire that has alternately been provoked and repressed in him. Now indeed it is a completely
detached thing which does not belong to any woman. He has
almost entirely succeeded in de-personalizing it. That is why he
feels that he can let it run its course. But not in any personal way.

He did not feel that he wanted marriage with Miriam. He wished
he did. He would have given his head to have felt a joyous desire
to marry her and to have her. Then why couldn't he bring it off?
There was some obstacle; and what was the obstacle? It lay in the

physical bondage. He shrank from the physical contact. But why? With her he felt bound up inside himself. He could not go out to her. Something struggled in him, but he could not get to her. Why? (ch. XI).

And Miriam does not insist upon marriage, she is willing to try out their feelings for each other. Theirs is a pitiful love-making. He cannot bear the blaze of love in her eyes; it is as if he must first draw a veil over her face and forget her. 'If he were really with her, he had to put aside himself and his desire. If he would have her, he had to put her aside.' Love brings him only a sense of death: 'He was a youth no longer. But why had he the dull pain in his soul? Why did the thought of death, the after-life, seem so sweet and consoling?' Love has brought them no satisfaction, only bitterness and disillusion. He turns back to his men friends and to Clara's company and the old quarrel between him and Miriam breaks out afresh. He decides to break off his relations with her. But at last he is to hear the truth about himself from Miriam. 'Always – it has been so!' she cried. 'It has been one long battle between us – you fighting away from me.' He tries to tell her that they have had some perfect hours. But she knows that these do not make up the healthy continuity of life. 'Always, from the very beginning – always the same!' She has called him a child of four. It is the truth, and it goes to the heart of his vanity. She has treated him as a mother treats a perverse child. He cannot stand it. 'He hated her. All these years she had treated him as if he were a hero, and thought of him secretly as an infant, a foolish child. Then why had she left the foolish child to his folly? His heart was hard against her' (ch. XI).

The full flood of his passion, freed of some of its incubus through his experience with Miriam, now turns to Clara. He tries to wear it out on her in the same impersonal way, and for a time lives in sheer physical ecstasy. With her at least he has had some solace, some relief. His mother has not stood so much between them. But it is only temporary, he cannot give himself to Clara any more than he could give himself to Miriam. Clara loves him or would love him if he could only rise above the mere passion that threw them together. '"I feel," she continued slowly, "as if

I hadn't got you, as if all of you weren't there, and as if it weren't *me* you were taking—" "Who then?" "Something just for yourself. It has been fine, so that I daren't think of it. But is it me you want, or is it *It?*" He again felt guilty. Did he leave Clara out of count and take simply woman? But he thought that was splitting a hair.' They begin to drift apart. He rehearses his old difficulties with his mother. 'I feel sometimes as if I wronged my women, mother.' But he doesn't know why.

'I even love Clara, and I did Miriam; but to give myself to them in marriage I couldn't. I couldn't belong to them. They seem to want *me*, and I can't ever give it them.'

'You haven't met the right woman.'

'And I never shall meet the right woman while you live.'

(ch. XIII)

His relations with Clara have brought about a marked change in Paul's attitude towards his mother. It is as if he realized at last that she is destroying his life's happiness. 'Then sometimes he hated her, and pulled at her bondage. His life wanted to free itself of her. It was like a circle where life wanted to turn back upon itself, and got no further. She bore him, loved him, kept him, and his love turned back into her, so that he could not be free to go forward with his own life, really love another woman.' But his realization, as far as it goes, brings no new initiative. He is twenty-four years old now but he still sums up his ambition as before: 'Go somewhere in a pretty house near London with my mother.'

The book now rounds out with the death of Paul's mother. Mrs Morel gradually wastes away with a slow and changeful illness; it is an incurable tumour, with great pain. Paul takes charge and never leaves his mother until the end. Their intimacy is occasionally disturbed by the clumsy intrusion of Morel, whose presence merely serves to irritate his wife. Paul and she commune with the old tenderness. 'Her blue eyes smiled straight into his, like a girl's — warm, laughing with tender love. It made him pant with terror, agony, and love.' Their reserve drops before the imminence of death, it seems as if they would be frank at last. But there is also the old constraint. 'They were both afraid of the veils that were ripping between them.' He suffers intensely. 'He felt as if his life were being destroyed, piece by piece, within him.' But mingled with his love and his anguish at her suffering there now enters a new feeling: the wish that she should die. Something in him wants her to die; seeing that she cannot live he would free both her and himself by hastening her death. So he gradually cuts down her nourishment and increases the deadliness of her medicine. Here again he approaches close to the source of his trouble; he dimly realizes that he has never lived outside of his mother and therefore has never really lived. The feeling that he cannot live without her and the feeling that he cannot live a life of his own as long as she is alive, here run side by side. But when the death which he himself has hastened overtakes her, he cries with a lover's anguish: "My love – my love – oh, my love!" he whispered again and again. "My love – oh, my love!"

But death has not freed Paul from his mother. It has completed his allegiance to her. For death has merely removed the last earthly obstacle to their ideal union; now he can love her as Dante loved his Beatrice. He avows his faithfulness to her by breaking off with the only two other women who have meant anything to him. He is completely resigned, life and death are no longer distinguished in his thinking. Life for him is only where his mother is and she is dead. So why live? He cannot answer, life has become contradictory. 'There seemed no reason why people should go along the street, and houses pile up in the daylight. There seemed no reason why these things should occupy the space, instead of leaving it empty. . . . He wanted everything to stand still, so that he could be with her again.' But life in him is just a hair stronger than death. 'He would not say it. He would not admit that he wanted to die, to have done. He would not own that life had beaten him, or that death had beaten him' (ch. xv).

The last chapter of the book is called 'Derelict'. The title emphasizes Mr Lawrence's already unmistakable meaning. Paul is adrift now; with the death of his mother he has lost his only mooring in life. There is no need to follow him further; when he is through despairing he will hope again and when he has compared one woman to his mother and found her wanting, he will

go on to another, in endless repetition. The author's final picture
of Paul's state of mind is full of seductive eloquence:

There was no Time, only Space. Who could say his mother had
lived and did not live? She had been in one place and was in
another; that was all. And his soul could not leave her, wherever
she was. Now she was gone abroad into the night, and he was with
her still. They were together. But yet there was his body, his
chest, that leaned against the stile, his hands on the wooden bar.
They seemed something. Where was he? – one tiny upright
speck of flesh, less than an ear of wheat lost in the field. He could
not bear it. On every side the immense dark silence seemed
pressing him, so tiny a spark, into extinction, and yet, almost
nothing, he could not be extinct. Night, in which everything was
lost, went reaching out, beyond stars and sun. Stars and sun, a
few bright grains, went spinning round for terror, and holding
each other in embrace, there in a darkness that outpassed them
all, and left them tiny and daunted. So much, and himself, infinitesimal, at the core a nothingness, and yet not nothing.

'Mother!' he whispered – 'mother!' (ch. xv)

### III

Such is the condensed account of Paul's love-life. Textual testimony could hardly go further to show that Paul loved his mother
too dearly. And shall we now say that it was *because* Mrs Morel
lavished all her affection upon her son? But then, most mothers
lavish a good deal of affection upon their sons and it is only
natural for sons to love their mothers dearly. Why should an
excess of these sacred sentiments produce such devastating results?
For it is undoubtedly the intention of the author to show us Paul
as a wreck and a ruin, a man damned out of all happiness at the
age of twenty-five, who has barely the strength left to will not to
die. And why should we accept as a type this man who seems to
bear so many ear-marks of degeneracy and abnormal impulse,
who is alternately a ruthless egotist and a vicious weakling in his
dealings with women, and who in the end stoops to shorten
the life of his own mother? Surely the thing is deeper and due to
profounder causes. But of these the author gives us no indication.

Let us therefore assume for the moment that Paul is by no means a degenerate, but merely an exaggeration of the normal, unhealthily nursed into morbid manifestations by an abnormal environment. If that can be established it may very well be that the story of Paul's love-life simply throws into high relief an intimate and constant relation between parent and child the significance of which has hitherto escaped general observation. Perhaps all men have something of Paul in them. In that case their instinctive recognition of their kinship with the hero of the book would go a great way towards explaining the potency of *Sons and Lovers*. We are fond of saying something like that about Hamlet.

The theory which would enable us to assume such a point of view is at once concrete, humanly understandable, and capable of personal verification. For Freud holds that the love instinct, whose sudden efflorescence after the age of puberty is invested with so much poetic charm, is not a belated endowment, but comes as the result of a gradual development which we can trace step by step from our earliest childhood. In fact, according to Freud, the evolution of the mature love instinct begins as soon as the child has sufficiently developed a sense of the otherness of its surroundings to single out its mother as the object of its affections. At first this is entirely instinctive and unconscious and comes as the natural result of the child's dependence upon its mother for food, warmth and comfort. We come preciously close to being born lovers. The mother is the one overwhelming presence of those earliest days, the source from which all good things flow, so that childhood is full of the sense of the mother's omnipotence. From her we first learn how to express affection, and the maternal caresses and the intimate feeling of oneness which we get from her form the easy analogies to love when we feel a conscious passion for another individual of the opposite sex. Our mother is, in a very real sense of the word, our first love.

As soon as the child is capable of making comparisons with other people it proceeds to celebrate the superiorities of its mother. She is the most beautiful, the most accomplished, the most powerful, and no other child's mother can equal her. But meanwhile the influence of the father, that other major constellation of our childhood, is also felt. Though not so gracious, he too is mighty, mightier than the mother, since he dominates her. His presence brings about a striking change in the attitude of the child, according to its sex. The boy, seeing that the mother loves the father, strives to be like him, in order to draw the mother's affection to himself. He takes his father as an ideal and sets about to imitate his masculine qualities. And the girl, becoming aware of the father's love for the mother, tries to attract some of his love to herself by imitating the mother. This is the process of self-identification which is already conditioned by the natural physical similarity where parent and child are of the same sex. Father and son, and mother and daughter, now have a common object of affection. But to the child this means at the same time an active rivalry, for the child is an unbridled egotist, intent upon nothing less than the exclusive possession of the affection of the beloved parent. It therefore manifests unmistakable signs of jealousy, even of frank hostility. So strong is this feeling that a careful examination of the unconscious childhood memories of thousands of individuals, such as is possible with the Freudian method of psychoanalysis, has yet to reveal an infancy in which a death phantasy about the rival parent has not played a part. The childish wish is ruthlessly realized in imagination; the boy suddenly dreams of living in a cottage with his mother after the father, let us say, has been devoured by the lion of last week's circus, while the girl revels in the thought of keeping house for her father after the mother has been conveniently removed. We may feel, then, that we were fellow conspirators with Paul when he prayed to God to have his father slain. For we have had the same wish in common: to eliminate the rival and celebrate a childish marriage with the parent of our choice.

From this naïve attitude the child is normally weaned by the maturing influences of education and by the absolute barriers which its childish wish encounters. It is a slow and gradual process of transference, which continues through childhood and puberty. The child is tenaciously rooted in its parents and does not easily relinquish its hold upon them. Even after it has acquired a dawning sense of the meaning of sex it continues to interweave its immature phantasies of procreation with its former ideal adoration of the parent. Thus the girl, having had a glimmering that the father has had something essential to do with her birth, may assign to him a similar function in regard to her dolls, which of course are her children. And the boy, similarly aware that his father has played a mysterious part with regard to the mother when she suddenly introduces another child into the nursery, is likely to usurp the exercise of this function to himself. Both substitutions are merely more sophisticated ways of eliminating the rival parent by making him unnecessary. It must be remembered, of course, that the child can have none of our reservations as to the direction which the erotic impulse may take, and therefore quite innocently directs its crude and imperfect erotic feelings towards its parent, from whom they must then be deflected. This is most favourably accomplished when there are other children in the family. The girl is quick to see the father in her brother and the boy transfers his worship of the mother to his sister. The father's manly qualities are used by the girl to embellish the brother when she sets him up as a love ideal. From him again she slowly extends her love phantasies to other boys of his and her acquaintance. The boy on his part, dowers his sister with the borrowed attributes of his mother and then passes from her to other girls who in turn are selected on the basis of their similarity to the sister and to the mother. In default of brothers or sisters other playmates have to serve the same purpose. The enforced quest of a love object other than the parent thus becomes the great incentive of our social radiation towards other individuals and to the world at large.

This process of deflection and transference, which is one of the main psychic labors of childhood, is facilitated by a parallel process that constantly represses a part of our thoughts to the unconscious. The mechanism of repression, as the Freudian psychology describes it, does not become operative until the age of about four or five, for at first the child does not repress at all and therefore has no unconscious. But the function of education consists largely in imposing innumerable taboos upon the child and in teaching it to respect the thou-shalt-nots. Thoughts and feelings such as the cruder egotistical impulses and the associations with bodily functions, which seem quite natural to the child's primitive and necessarily unmoral mind, gradually fall under the cultural ban proclaimed by parents and educators, so that the unconscious becomes a receptacle for all the thoughts that are rendered painful and disagreeable by the slowly developing sense of shame and of moral and ethical behaviour. We 'put away childish things' by putting them into the unconscious. Our germinating sexual ideas and our naïve erotic attitude towards our parents become particularly 'impermissible' and we therefore draw an especially heavy veil of forgetfulness over this part of our childhood. But though we can forget, we cannot obliterate, and the result.of this early fixation upon our parents is to leave in our mind an indelible imprint, or 'imago', of both our mother and our father. Our parents are always with us in our unconscious. They become our ultimate criterion by which we judge men and women, and exercise the most potent influence upon our love choice. The imago of them that holds us to our unconscious allegiance is a picture, not as we know them later, old and declining, but as we saw them first, young and radiant, and dowered, as it seemed to us then, with godlike gifts. We cannot go on loving them so we do the next best thing; the boy chooses a woman who resembles his mother as closely as possible, and the girl mates with the man who reminds her most of her father.

Such, according to Freud, is the psychological genesis of the emotion of love. The normal evolution of love from the first maternal caress is finally accomplished when the individual definitely transfers his allegiance to a self-chosen mate and thereby steps out of the charmed family circle in which he has been held from infancy. That this is difficult even under normal circumstance seems already to have been recognized in the Bible, where Christ says with so much solemnity: 'For this cause shall a man leave father and mother'; as if only so weighty a reason could induce a child to leave its parents. Freud, in postulating the above development as the norm, proceeds to attach grave and far-reaching consequences to any deviations from this standard.

The effect of any disturbance in the balanced and harmonious influence of both parents upon the child, or of any abnormal pressure of circumstances or wilful action that forces the child into a specialized attitude toward either parent, is subtly and unerringly reproduced in the later love-life. The reader himself will probably recall from his own observation, a large number of cases where the love-life has been thwarted, or stunted, or never expressed. He will think of those old bachelors whose warm attachment to their mother has so much superficial charm, as well as of those old maids who so self-effacingly devote themselves to their fathers. He will also recall that almost typical man whose love interest persistently goes where marriage is impossible, preferably to a woman already pre-empted by another man or to a much older woman, so that his love can never come to rest in its object; he will wonder whether this man too is not preserving his ideal allegiance to his mother by avoiding that final detachment from her which marriage would bring. He will notice a class of men and women who, even though their parents are dead, seem to have resigned marriage and live in a kind of small contentment with a constantly narrowing horizon. Or he may know of actual marriages that are unhappy because the memory of one of the parents has not been sufficiently laid to rest, and the joke about the mother-in-law or the pie that mother used to make, will acquire a new significance for him. And to all these cases thousands must still be added where neurotic and hysteric patients reveal with unmistakable clearness that the ghosts of the parents still walk about in the troubled psyches of these unfortunates, influencing life and happiness with paralyzing effect. These are all manifestations which the reader hitherto has observed only as results, without knowing the causes or trying to ascertain them. With the aid of the Freudian theory such examples may now help him to see, as perhaps he has already begun to see in Paul, the tremendous rôle that the abnormal fixation upon the parent plays in the psychic development of the individual. And in so doing he may perhaps also gain some insight into the part that his own parents have played in his normal psychic growth, just as disease gives us a clearer understanding of health or as

Madame Montessori's study of subnormal children has enabled
her to formulate general laws of education.

## IV

We can now return to *Sons and Lovers* with a new understanding.
Why has the attitude of the son to his mother here had such a
devastating effect upon his whole life? Why could he not overcome this obstacle like other children and ultimately attain some
measure of manhood? Why, in short, was the surrender so complete? In Paul's case the abnormal fixation upon the mother is
most obviously conditioned by the father, whose unnatural
position in the family is responsible for the distortion of the
normal attitude of the child towards its parents. The father
ideal simply does not exist for Paul; where there should have
been an attractive standard of masculinity to imitate, he can only
fear and despise. The child's normal dependence upon the mother
is perpetuated because there is no counter-influence to detach it
from her. But there is another distortion, equally obvious, which
fatally influences the natural development. Paul's early fixation
upon his mother is met and enhanced by Mrs Morel's abnormally
concentrated affection for her son. Her unappeased love, which
can no longer go out towards her husband, turns to Paul for
consolation; she *makes* him love her too well. Her love becomes
a veritable Pandora's box of evil. For Paul is now hemmed in
on all sides by too much love and too much hate.

If now we compare Paul's boyhood and adolescence with,
let us say, the reader's own, we find that the difference is, to a
great extent, one of consciousness and unconsciousness. All those
psychic processes which are usually unconscious or at least
heavily veiled in the normal psycho-sexual development lie close
to consciousness in Paul and break through into his waking
thoughts at every favorable opportunity. Everything is raw and
exposed in him and remains so, kept quick to the touch by the
pressure of an abnormal environment which instead of moulding,
misshapes him. The normal hostility towards the father which is
conditioned in every boy by a natural jealousy of the mother's

affection, is nursed in him to a conscious hate through Morel's actual brutality and his mother's undisguised bitterness and contempt. And the normal love for the mother which ordinarily serves as a model for the man's love for other women is in him perverted into abnormal expression almost at his mother's breast, so that he is always conscious of his infatuation with his mother and can never free his love-making from that paralyzing influence. These powerful determinants of the love-life which we acquire from our parents would be too overwhelming in every case were it not for the process of submersion or repression already referred to. This repression usually sets in at an early stage of childhood and acts biologically as a protective mechanism by allowing us to develop a slowly expanding sense of selfhood through which we gradually differentiate ourselves from our parents. In this way the fateful dominance of the parents is broken, though their influence remains in the unconscious as a formative and directing impulse.

In Paul this salutary process never takes place because he cannot free himself from the incubus of his parents long enough to come to some sense of himself. He remains enslaved by his parent complex instead of being moulded and guided by it. One turns back to that astonishing scene at Lincoln Cathedral. Here Paul goes to the roots of his mother's hold upon him. For his passionate reproaches hurled at his mother because she has lost her youth, prove that the mother-imago, in all its pristine magic, has never diminished its sway over him; he has never been able to forget or to subordinate that first helpless infatuation. If only she could be young again so that he could remain her child-lover! With that thought and wish so conscious in him nothing else in life can become really desirable, and all initiative is dried up at the source. Paul cannot expand towards the universe in normal activity and form an independent sex interest because for him his mother has become the universe; she stands between him and life and the other woman. There is a kind of bottomless childishness about him; life in a pretty house with his mother – the iteration sounds like a childish prattle. Miriam feels it when she calls him a child of four which she can no longer nurse. Nor can

Clara help him by becoming a wanton substitute for his mother. Only the one impossible ideal holds him, and that means the constant turning in upon himself which is death. Paul goes to pieces because he can never make the mature sexual decision away from his mother, he can never accomplish the physical and emotional transfer.

If now this striking book, taken as it stands, bears such unexpected witness to the truth of Freud's remarkable psychosexual theory, it is at least presumable that the author himself and the rest of his work also stand in some very definite relation to this theory. The feeling that *Sons and Lovers* must be autobiographical is considerably strengthened by the somewhat meagre personal detail which Mr Edwin Björkman supplies in an introduction to Mr Lawrence's first play. Mr Lawrence was himself the son of a collier in the Derbyshire coal-mining district and his mother seems to have occupied an exceptional position in the family, showing herself to be a woman of great fortitude and initiative, who evidently dominated the household. Mr Björkman is silent concerning the father, but gives us the interesting information that *Sons and Lovers* was written not long after the mother's death. This information is not sufficient, however, to warrant our inquiry going beyond the author's writings, a step for which, in any case, it would be necessary to have both his permission and his cooperation. We must therefore limit ourselves to the testimony of Mr Lawrence's work. This consists of two additional novels, a volume of poems, and a play. What is truly astonishing is that all of these, in various disguises and transparent elaborations, hark back to the same problem: the direct and indirect effects of an excessive maternal allegiance and the attempt to become emancipated from it.

Reference has already been made to the poems. This is the way the author ends a love poem:

> What else – it is perfect enough,
> It is perfectly complete,
> You and I,
> What more – ?
> *Strange, how we suffer in spite of this!*

Why, it may well be asked, should the perfection of love bring suffering? Certainly the love poems of adolescence are not as a rule colored with the feeling of suffering as unmotivated as this. But there is a second poem, entitled 'End of Another Home Holiday' which in the short space of three pages states Paul's whole problem with unmistakable precision. The poet tells how dearly he loves his home and then continues as follows:

> The light has gone out from under my mother's door.
>> That she should love me so,
>> She, so lonely, greying now,
>> And I leaving her,
>> Bent on my pursuits!

How curiously that last line comes in, 'Bent on my pursuits!' as if he felt that he ought to stay at home. Here we have again the son who cannot leave his mother; the mere thought of doing so fills him with self-reproach. In the next few lines the reproach deepens:

> Forever, ever by my shoulder pitiful Love will linger,
> Crouching as little houses crouch under the mist when I
> turn.
> Forever, out of the mist, the church lifts up a reproachful
> finger,
> Pointing my eyes in wretched defiance where love hides
> her face to mourn.

Even inanimate things point the finger of reproach at him. A little later in the same poem the mother becomes a symbolic figure, following the son through life like a Norn, as she begs for his love.

> While ever at my side,
>> Frail and sad, with grey, bowed head,
>> The beggar-woman, the yearning-eyed
>> Inexorable love goes lagging.

. . .

> But when I draw the scanty cloak of silence over my eyes,
> Piteous Love comes peering under the hood;
> Touches the clasp with trembling fingers, and tries
> To put her ears to the painful sob of my blood;
> While her tears soak through to my breast,
>> Where they burn and cauterize.

The poem ends with the call of the corncrake in the poet's ear, crying monotonously:

> With a piteous, unalterable plaint, that deadens
>   My confident activity:
> With a hoarse, insistent request that falls
>   Unweariedly, unweariedly,
>   Asking something more of me,
>     Yet more of me!

An interesting, tell-tale clew in these last lines shows how thoroughly this poem is Paul's and to how great an extent Paul and the author are one and the same. For the careful reader will remember that Paul too, coming home over the fields after visiting Miriam is strongly depressed by the call of this same little bird and immediately goes in to his mother to tell her that he still loves her best and that he has broken off with Miriam. Has not his mother too, 'deadened his confident activity'. Her influence could hardly be better described in a single phrase. The whole poem is a protest against the terrible allegiance that the mother exacts, just as Paul, towards the end of the book, reproaches his mother for the failure of his life. It can hardly be doubted that a vital part of the lyricist has gone into Paul.

In reading the two remaining novels and the play our attention is immediately struck by a curious sameness and limitation of motif that underlies them all. In each there is a deadly father or husband hate, a poignant sense of death, and a picture of marriage or love that does not satisfy. Siegmund, the husband in *The Trespasser*, is exposed to a hate so withering that he collapses before it. He is a kind and gentle musician, too effeminate for a man, and entirely devoid of initiative. The hatred of his wife and children is practically unmotivated, we are simply asked to assume it in order to follow him in his affair with Helena. This brings him no solace, he cannot come to rest in her, his love for her simply brings him the sense of death. It is the psychology of Paul transferred to a man of forty, and Helena's struggle to make his love for her real is much like Miriam's. In the play, *The Widowing of Mrs Holroyd*, the wife seeks to escape from a brutal and drunken husband by eloping with another man. The death of her husband in a mining accident intervenes and brings her a sense of pity and remorse because she never tried to win and hold her husband's love. She had married him without love. Her son hates his father and wishes him dead. Blackmore, the man with whom she wanted to elope, has much of Paul in him; his belief that love can bring happiness is never more than half-hearted. The sense of guilt that the death of the husband brings to both of them, makes the elopement impossible. Death always supervenes upon the impermissible with Mr Lawrence.

In *The White Peacock* the background is again a ruthless hate for the husband and father. One of the daughters says: 'There is always a sense of death in this house. I believe my mother hated my father before I was born. That was death in her veins for me before I was born. It makes a difference.' We get a picture of women who marry meaningless husbands and men who marry unsatisfying wives. Lettie marries Leslie because George, whom she really loves, lacks the initiative to claim her, and George marries Meg after his abortive love for Lettie has made him despair of life. Neither he nor she come to any emotional satisfaction; Lettie consoles herself for her aimlessly empty husband by living in her children, and George ends his 'Liebestod' in drink. Lettie's brother, who tells the story, is almost sexless except towards his sister, whom he admires like a lover. One gradually gets a sense of monotony; happiness in love is always impossible in this fictional world of Mr Lawrence, and hate for the parent or husband is the master passion. The motivation is often indistinct or inadequate in all three stories, and the artistry is inferior. They were evidently only preludes to *Sons and Lovers*.

In the story of Paul the author has reached the final expression of a problem which haunts his every effort. The creative labour of self-realization which makes *Sons and Lovers* such a priceless commentary on the love-life of today, accomplished itself but slowly in Mr Lawrence, waiting, no doubt, for his artistic maturity and the final clarity which the death of his mother must have brought. And if, as I have tried to show, he has been able, though unknowingly, to attest the truth of what is perhaps the most far-reaching psychological theory ever propounded, he has also given us an illuminating insight into the mystery of artistic creation. For Mr Lawrence has escaped the destructive fate that dogs the hapless Paul by the grace of expression: out of the dark struggles of his own soul he has emerged as a triumphant artist. In every epoch the soul of the artist is sick with the problems of his generation. He cures himself by expression in his art. And by producing a catharsis in the spectator through the enjoyment of his art he also heals his fellow beings. His artistic stature is measured by the universality of the problem which his art has transfigured.

# J. Middleton Murry

## SON AND LOVER (1931)

*Sons and Lovers* has a double riches: as the intimate life-history of the youth of a genius, and as a significant act. The significance of the act of writing the book will only be fully apparent when we have considered the life-history which it records.

Lawrence was born on 11 September 1885, the fourth child of a collier father and bourgeoise mother. The father was almost the pure animal, in the good and bad senses of the phrase: warm, quick, careless, irresponsible, living in the moment and a liar. The mother was responsible, and 'heroic'. In *Sons and Lovers* Lawrence makes a great effort to hold the balance fairly between them. Not being God, he found the task impossible. He would have liked to excuse the father, to make the mother bear some part of the blame for the father's slow disintegration.

The pity was, she was too much his opposite. She could not be content with the little he might be; she would have him the much that he ought to be. So, in seeking to make him nobler than he could be, she destroyed him. She injured and hurt and scarred herself, but she lost none of her worth.

But not to have 'destroyed' him in this recondite sense would have meant to be destroyed herself, and not only herself, but her children also. To seek, as she did, 'to make him undertake his own responsibilities, to make him fulfil his obligations' was not an encroachment, but a sheer necessity. Had she been less his opposite, she might indeed have suffered less, but the family would have collapsed upon itself. In the last issue, the father was responsible. Lawrence declared it again in the *Fantasia*.

So the mother withdrew from the father. There was no help for it. The essential estrangement had happened before Lawrence was born. She had not desired his coming, as she had desired the coming at least of the first of the two brothers before him. A lovely and tender passage of the book describes the sudden birth of her devouring love for the frail little boy, with blue eyes like her own (ch. ii).

This, if it is wholly imagination – which it is probably not, for there must have been little of her inward history which Lawrence's mother did not eventually confide in him – is an imagination we can trust as truth. The sudden resolve of her heart was fulfilled, and lavishly. She 'made it up' in love a hundredfold to the child. He became, as was inevitable in such a case, abnormally sensitive. He expanded preternaturally in this warm atmosphere of love. His capacity for experience was unusually great, so likewise was his shrinking from it. A hungry desire for contact of the same intimate kind as that which he and his mother lavished upon each other was counterpoised by an anguished fear of it. At fourteen, 'he was a rather small and rather finely-made boy, with dark brown hair and light blue eyes. His face was becoming . . . rough-featured, almost rugged . . . and it was extraordinarily mobile.'

Usually he looked as if he saw things, was full of life, and warm; then his smile, like his mother's, came suddenly and was very lovable; and then, when there was any clog in his soul's quick running, his face went stupid and ugly. He was the sort of boy that becomes a clown and a lout as soon as he is not understood, or feels himself held cheap; and, again, is adorable at the first touch of warmth.

He suffered very much from the first contact with anything. When he was seven, the starting school had been a nightmare and a torture to him. But afterwards he liked it. (ch. v)

Those who knew Lawrence well as a man will recognize immediately the truth of this picture of him as a boy. That *is* the boy who became the man they knew.

He grew with his soul sensitized utterly to the determination and the suffering of his mother in the long, unending struggle with her husband. Fortunately for him, it was not a silent and suppressed struggle such as so often, in a like situation, undermines the inmost being of an uncomprehending child. The antagonism was manifest and violent; more terrifying, but less subtly disintegrating. There were outbursts of drunkenness and downright brutality on the father's part, and they were fearful; but they belonged to a child's world. They were plain and elemental. The father does not come home from the pit: his dinner waits, the potatoes go dry. A hundred to one he has stayed drinking at the public house; but there is the agonising chance that something bad may have happened in the pit. If he comes home with too much beer in him, it will be bad; if he is brought home on a stretcher, or jolted off over the cobbles in the ambulance to the hospital, it will be worse. Or perhaps, if the injury is not too bad, it may be better. For there is the club money, and the ten shillings a week that the men of his stall put aside, which together makes more than the twenty-five shillings he has been giving lately. And, if it is beer, the worst won't happen, for he is in his heart afraid of mother. But then, once or twice, he has done evil things – cut her head open by flinging a drawer at her. There is still the fear. The children listen, with indrawn breath and thumping hearts, to the angry voices contending, one hot, one cold in anger, mingled inextricably and for ever with the shrieking of the ash-tree in the wind.

A fearful childhood, judged from one point of view, but from another how rich in the elemental drama that a child could understand and a man never forget! The issue how simple, manifest as the stars! The call upon the children the deepest their souls could sustain. They cleaved like little champions to their mother; they despised their father. And he, who knew that they were right to despise him, who knew that 'he had denied the God in him', rotted in his own isolation.

That his father 'had denied the God in him' was Lawrence's verdict also in the *Fantasia*; but then it was a still more advised pronouncement. Morel refused to take 'the next creative step into the future'. It was not an inordinate demand; for Morel the creative step consisted simply in taking responsibility for his children, in being in act, not merely in name, a father, in becoming a man whom his wife must respect and could not despise. He made not even a faint attempt; he slunk away. Inevitably, the mother's starved spirit sought satisfaction through her sons; and two of them, the eldest and the youngest, responded wholly to her call. When the eldest died, evidently on the threshold of a brilliantly successful career, the youngest son became her 'man'. As his great namesake had said, 'Whatever I do, I do it unto the Lord', so Paul Morel could have said, 'Whatever I do, I do it unto my mother.' She was to live the life of which she had been cheated, through him; he would bring her the spiritual fulfilment she longed for. He had no ambition for himself, but all for her.

*Sons and Lovers* is the story of Paul Morel's desperate attempts to break away from the tie that was strangling him. All unconsciously, his mother had roused in him the stirrings of sexual desire; she had, by the sheer intensity of her diverted affection made him a man before his time. He felt for his mother what he should have felt for the girl of his choice. Let us be clear, as Lawrence himself tried to be clear in the *Fantasia*. Lawrence was not, so far as we can tell, sexually precocious; he was spiritually precocious. We are told that Paul Morel remained virgin till twenty-three. But his spiritual love for his mother was fully developed long before. What could be more poignant, or in implication more fearful, than the story he tells of the illness which fell upon him at sixteen? (He had told the same story before, in *The Trespasser*; it was a crucial happening in his boyhood.)

Paul was very ill. His mother lay in bed at nights with him; they could not afford a nurse. He grew worse, and the crisis approached. One night he tossed into consciousness in the ghastly, sickly feeling of dissolution, when all the cells in the body seem in intense irritability to be breaking down, and consciousness makes a last flare of struggle, like madness.

'I s'll die, mother!' he cried, heaving for breath on the pillow. She lifted him up, crying in a small voice:

'Oh, my son – my son!'

That brought him to. He realized her. His whole will rose up and arrested him. He put his head on her breast, and took ease of her for love. (ch. VI)

It is terribly poignant, and terribly wrong. Almost better that a boy should die than have such an effort forced upon him by such means. He is called upon to feel in full consciousness for his mother all that a full-grown man might feel for the wife of his bosom.

In this same year, when Lawrence was sixteen, he met the girl Miriam, whose destiny was to be linked with his own for the next ten years, until his mother's death. He also met the farm and the family of which Miriam was the daughter. It became a second home to him. Beautifully situated in a valley about three miles away from the miner's cottage in Eastwood, the small decaying farm, with its pastures nibbled by rabbits to the quick, gave him the full freedom of that natural life which was always washing to the edge of the mining village. There he found the richness of life without which he wilted. He became as one of the family, and the Leivers' kitchen more dear to him than his own.

Miriam was about the same age as himself, perhaps a year younger, when Lawrence met her. She encouraged, stimulated, and appreciated his gifts; she saw in him the wonderful being that he was, and she had fallen in love with him long before he with her. She was free to fall in love; he was not. So that when we say that Lawrence fell in love with Miriam, we mean that had he been free, and not bound, and ever more deliberately and tightly bound, he might have fallen in love with her, as she undoubtedly did with him. He fell in love with her only so far as he was capable of falling in love.

The history is painful. In *Sons and Lovers*, Lawrence tells it as though Miriam failed him; and he tried, even at the end of his life in *Lady Chatterley's Lover*, to tell the story thus.

I held forth with rapture to her, positively with rapture. I simply went up in smoke. And she adored me. The serpent in the grass was sex. She somehow didn't have any, at least not where it's supposed to be. I got thinner and crazier. Then I said we'd got to be lovers. I talked her into it. So she let me. I was excited, and she never wanted it. She adored me, she loved me to talk to her and kiss her; in that way she had a passion for me. But the other she just didn't want. And there are lots of women like her. And it was just the other that I *did* want. So there we split. I was cruel and left her.

Lawrence at all times needed desperately to convince himself in this matter of Miriam, and to the end he did not succeed. He does not tell the truth in *Sons and Lovers*, still less in *Lady Chatterley*: he comes closest to the truth in the *Fantasia*. Actually, while his mother still lived, he was incapable of giving to another woman the love without which sexual possession must be a kind of violence done: done not to the woman only, but also and equally to the man: above all to a man like Lawrence. All his life long Lawrence laboured to convince himself, and other people, that sexual desire carried with it its own validity: that the spiritual and the sexual were distinct. In fact, he never could believe it. What he did believe was something quite different, and quite true, namely that, in a man and woman who are whole, as he never was whole, the spiritual and the sexual might be one. This he declared in *Fantasia*, and yet again with his latest breath, in *The Escaped Cock*. He believed in a harmony which it was impossible for him personally to achieve, without a physical resurrection.

So saying, we anticipate: but it is essential to grasp as clearly as we can the subtle human tragedy of the affair with Miriam. It was the tragedy of Lawrence's entry into sexual life, and it haunted him all his days. In *Sons and Lovers* he conceals the truth. He cannot endure really to face it in consciousness. The story told there is subtly inconsistent with itself. At one moment comes a gleam of full recognition, as when he says of his mother: 'She bore him, loved him, kept him, and his love turned back into her, so that he could not be free to go forward with his own life, really love another woman.' But as he tells the story of the passion itself, he represents that it is not himself, but Miriam who is at fault. She is frigid, she shrinks from sexual passion; and this may have been true in part. But the truth was only partial. When later Lawrence came to a woman who was not frigid, the failure, though long drawn out, was more painful still. In representing that the fault was Miriam's, Lawrence wronged her.

But we have to remember that *Sons and Lovers* was written after the death of his mother at a moment when Lawrence believed that he had attained sexual fulfilment. If he had not attained it with Miriam, he had some faint excuse for thinking that the fault was hers. He felt that it was not his own fault, and he had good reason for that. Nevertheless, it was his duty in *Sons and Lovers* to put the blame where it lay – if on a person at all, then upon his mother, who had taken from him that to which she had no right, and had used the full weight of her tremendous influence to prevent her son from giving to a woman the love which she so jealously guarded for herself. The fight was between his mother and Miriam, and it was an utterly unequal battle, between a strong and jealous woman and a diffident and unawakened girl.

In the story, Miriam is sacrificed, because Lawrence cannot tell the truth. Probably he could not tell it even to himself. The physical relation with Miriam was impossible. 'You will not easily get a man to believe', he wrote in *Fantasia*, 'that his carnal love for the woman he has made his wife is as high a love as that he felt for his mother.' If Lawrence could write that when he had found his wife, and when his mother had been dead ten years, what did he feel while his mother was still alive, and he was engaged in talking Miriam into being his lover? He might talk and talk, but how could he convince her of what he did not himself believe – namely, that it was good that she should yield herself to him. He was a divided man. His love and his passion were separated. And because his passion was separated from his love, his passion was not true passion; it had but half the man behind, and to his own thinking, the worse half. This was the poisoned sting. He was, in his own eyes, degrading her, and degrading himself by his demand upon her.

What there was between Miriam and himself was an intense spiritual communion, and mutual stimulation of the mind. Whether it would ever, or could ever, have ripened into love on his side, who can say? Whatever it might have been was cankered in the bud. But I do not believe it ever could have ripened; Lawrence's subsequent history makes that plain to me. Happiness in love was not in Lawrence's destiny.

The appeal he made to Miriam was to her charity. He needed the comfort of her body, and she yielded herself to the sacrifice.

She looked at him and was sorry for him; his eyes were dark with torture. She was sorry for him; it was worse for him to have this deflected love than for herself, who could never be properly mated. He was restless, for ever urging forward and trying to find a way out. He might do as he liked, and have what he liked of her. (ch. xi)

Paul did not want her, but, as Mellors says in *Lady Chatterley's Lover*, 'he wanted *it*'. Miriam did not want him, but she wanted to give him *it*, because he wanted it. The indulgence of their 'passion' was disastrous, because it was not passion at all. On both sides it was deliberate, and not passionate. Miriam's charity was passionate, but she had no sexual desire for Paul; Paul's need for the release and rest of sexual communion was passionate, but not his desire for Miriam. Each was a divided and tortured being. Miriam strove to subdue her body to her spirit, Paul strove to subdue his spirit to his body. They hurt themselves, and they hurt each other. Consider Lawrence's own words in *Sons and Lovers*:

A good many of the nicest men he knew were like himself, bound in by their own virginity, which they could not break out of. They were so sensitive to their women that they would go without them for ever rather than do them a hurt, an injustice. Being the sons of mothers whose husbands had blundered rather brutally through their feminine sanctities, they were themselves too diffident and shy. They could easier deny themselves than incur any reproach from a woman; for a woman was like their mother, and they were full of the sense of their mother. (ch. xi)

Yet Paul did the hurt, the injustice, to Miriam, and still more to himself in the process. And the hurt he does her and himself is more delicate than he can acknowledge here. He does not and cannot feel towards her what by his own standards he must feel in order to justify his demand of her. He sacrifices her, or allows her to sacrifice herself, and in so doing, he violates himself. And the consequence is disaster; for their 'passion' brings not the release from the torment of inward division which he seeks, but an exasperation of the torment.

From the new torment, new release is sought: and the appeal is always to the woman's charity. Clara Dawes is a married woman, where Miriam was virgin. It is easier for her to give, and easier for Paul to take. But the desire is not for the woman, but for release through the woman; and the woman gives not from desire but from pity.

He needed her badly. She had him in her arms, and he was miserable. With her warmth she folded him over, consoled him, loved him. . . . She could not bear the suffering in his voice. She was afraid in her soul. He might have anything of her – anything; but she did not want to *know*. She felt she could not bear it. She wanted him to be soothed upon her – soothed. She stood clasping him and caressing him, and he was something unknown to her – something almost uncanny. She wanted to soothe him into forgetfulness. . . . She knew how stark and alone he was, and she felt it was great that he came to her; and she took him simply because his need was bigger either than her or him. . . . She did this for him in his need. (ch. XIII)

At the crucial moment, we cannot distinguish between Clara and Miriam. One is married, one is virgin; but their attitude towards him is the same, the appeal he makes to them the same.

One's instinct shrinks from it all. It is all wrong, humanly wrong. This man, we feel, has no business with sex at all. He is born to be a saint: then let him be one, and become a eunuch for the sake of the Kingdom of Heaven. For him, we prophesy, sex must be one long laceration, one long and tortured striving for the unattainable. This feverish effort to become a man turns fatally upon itself; it makes him more a child than before. He struggles frenziedly to escape being child-man to his mother, and he becomes only child-man again to other women, and the first great bond is not broken. If the woman is virgin like Miriam, he breaks her, by communicating to her the agony of his own division; if the woman is married like Clara, she breaks him, by abasing him in his own eyes.

To love a woman, in the simplest and most universal sense of the word, was impossible to Lawrence while his mother lived. Whether it was possible afterwards, the event will show. It will need almost a miracle, if he is to find his sexual salvation; for the fearful phrase of his own later invention fits him. It should fit him. He made it for himself. He is a man who is 'crucified into sex', and he will carry the stigmata all his life.

Is it, we ask in pity and wonder, just a destiny? Is it simply that the sin of the father is visited through the mother upon the child? Was no escape possible? There is no answer to these questions; yet they return again and again to the mind. Surely, we say to ourselves, he could have broken that fearful bond that bound him to his mother. Was there not some ultimate weakness in the man that held him back? We may say that it was the terror of inflicting pain upon her. But there is a point at which the rarest and most tender virtue becomes a vice and a weakness; and perhaps to decide where that point lies is not so hard as it seems. When we begin to resent the compulsion of our virtues, they have become vices. Then the necessity of a choice and a decision is upon us: we must either cease to resent, or cease to obey, our virtues. Integrity lies either way. But to continue to obey, and to continue to resent – this means a cleavage which, once past a certain point, can never be healed again. Perhaps the final tragedy of Lawrence – and his life was finally a bitter tragedy – was that he could never make the choice on which his own integrity depended. To the end he resented his virtues, yet in act obeyed them, and in imagination blasphemed them.

Certainly, while his mother lived, until he himself was twenty-six, he resented the compulsion of his fear of paining her more and more deeply, yet he obeyed it. She was determined, consciously or unconsciously, that no woman save herself should have her son's love; and he obeyed her. What genuine and unhesitating passion there was in Lawrence's life before his mother's death went to a man, not a woman.

Miriam's eldest brother, the farmer's eldest son, Edgar Leivers of *Sons and Lovers*, George Saxton of *The White Peacock*, called forth in Lawrence something far more near to what most of us understand by passionate love than either Miriam or Clara.

Contact with Miriam made him glow with a kind of spiritual incandescence; they throbbed together in a tense vibration of soul, which Paul strove vainly to convert into a passion of the body. His passion for Clara was from the beginning a physical need. But for the original of George and Edgar he must have felt something for which the best name is the simple one of love. In *Sons and Lovers* this friendship is but lightly touched; in *The White Peacock* the tremor of authenticity is not to be mistaken. Cyril's love for George has more of reality in it than any of the love affairs in the book; it yields in convincingness only to the diffused yet passionate affection for the farm and all its inhabitants which is the real emotional substance of the story. . . .

# Mark Schorer

# TECHNIQUE AS DISCOVERY (1948)

MODERN criticism, through its exacting scrutiny of literary texts, has demonstrated with finality that in art beauty and truth are indivisible and one. The Keatsian overtones of these terms are mitigated and an old dilemma is solved if for beauty we substitute form, and for truth, content. We may, without risk of loss, narrow them even more, and speak of technique and subject matter. Modern criticism has shown us that to speak of content as such is not to speak of art at all, but of experience; and that it is only when we speak of the *achieved* content, the form, the work of art as a work of art, that we speak as critics. The difference between content, or experience, and achieved content, or art, is technique.

When we speak of technique, then, we speak of nearly everything. For technique is the means by which the writer's experience, which is his subject matter, compels him to attend to it; technique is the only means he has of discovering, exploring, developing his subject, of conveying its meaning, and, finally, of evaluating it. And surely it follows that certain techniques are sharper tools than others, and will discover more; that the writer capable of the most exacting technical scrutiny of his subject matter will produce works with the most satisfying content, works with thickness and resonance, works which reverberate, works with maximum meaning.[1]

We are no longer able to regard as seriously intended criticism of poetry which does not assume these generalizations; but the case for fiction has not yet been established. The novel is still read as though its content has some value in itself, as though the subject matter of fiction has greater or lesser value in itself, and as though technique were not a primary but a supplementary element, capable perhaps of not unattractive embellishments upon the surface of the subject, but hardly of its essence. Or technique is thought of in blunter terms than those which one associates with poetry, as such relatively obvious matters as the arrangement of events to create plot; or, within plot, of suspense and climax; or as the means of revealing character motivation, relationship, and development; or as the use of point of view, but point of view as some nearly arbitrary device for the heightening of dramatic interest through the narrowing or broadening of perspective upon the material, rather than as a means toward the positive definition of theme. As for the resources of language, these, somehow, we almost never think of as a part of the technique of fiction – language as used to create a certain texture and tone which in themselves state and define themes and meanings; or language, the counters of our ordinary speech, as forced, through conscious manipulation, into all those larger meanings which our ordinary speech almost never intends. Technique in fiction, all this is a way of saying, we somehow continue to regard as merely a means of organizing material which is 'given' rather than as the means of exploring and defining the values in an area of experience which, for the first time *then*, are being given.

Technique in fiction is, of course, all those obvious forms of it which are usually taken to be the whole of it, and many others; but for the present purposes, let it be thought of in two respects particularly: the uses to which language, as language, is put to express the quality of the experience in question; and the uses of point of view not only as a mode of dramatic delimitation, but more particularly, of thematic definition. Technique is really what T. S. Eliot means by 'convention' – any selection, structure, or distortion, any form or rhythm imposed upon the world of action; by means of which – it should be added – our apprehension of the world of action is enriched or renewed.[2] In this sense, everything is technique which is not the lump of experience itself, and one cannot properly say that a writer has no technique or that he eschews technique, for, being a writer, he cannot do so.

We can speak of good and bad technique, of adequate and inadequate, of technique which serves the novel's purpose, or disserves.

To say what one means in art is never easy, and the more intimately one is implicated in one's material, the more difficult it is. If, besides, one commits fiction to a therapeutic function which is to be operative not on the audience but on the author, declaring, as D. H. Lawrence did, that 'one sheds one's sicknesses in books, repeats and presents again one's emotions to be master of them', the difficulty is vast. It is an acceptable theory only with the qualification that technique, which objectifies, is under no other circumstances so imperative. For merely to repeat one's emotions, merely to look into one's heart and write, is also merely to repeat the round of emotional bondage. If our books are to be exercises in self-analysis, then technique must – and alone can – take the place of the absent analyst.

Lawrence, in the relatively late Introduction to his *Collected Poems*, made that distinction of the amateur between his 'real' poems and his 'composed' poems, between the poems which expressed his demon directly and created their own form 'willy-nilly', and the poems which, through the hocus pocus of technique, he spuriously put together and could, if necessary, revise. His belief in a 'poetry of the immediate present', poetry in which nothing is fixed, static, or final, where all is shimmeriness and impermanence and vitalistic essence, arose from this mistaken notion of technique. And from this notion, an unsympathetic critic like D. S. Savage can construct a case which shows Lawrence driven 'concurrently to the dissolution of personality and the dissolution of art'. The argument suggests that Lawrence's early, crucial novel, *Sons and Lovers*, is another example of meanings confused by an impatience with technical resources.

The novel has two themes: the crippling effects of a mother's love on the emotional development of her son; and the 'split' between kinds of love, physical and spiritual, which the son develops, the kinds represented by two young women, Clara and Miriam. The two themes should, of course, work together, the second being, actually, the result of the first: this 'split' is the 'crippling'. So one would expect to see the novel developed, and so Lawrence, in his famous letter to Edward Garnett, where he says that Paul is left at the end with the 'drift towards death', apparently thought he had developed it. Yet in the last few sentences of the novel, Paul rejects his desire for extinction and turns toward 'the faintly humming, glowing town', to life – as nothing in his previous history persuades us that he could unfalteringly do.

The discrepancy suggests that the book may reveal certain confusions between intention and performance.

The first of these is the contradiction between Lawrence's explicit characterizations of the mother and father and his tonal evaluations of them. It is a problem not only of style (of the contradiction between expressed moral epithets and the more general texture of the prose which applies to them) but of point of view. Morel and Lawrence are never separated, which is a way of saying that Lawrence maintains for himself in his book the confused attitude of his character. The mother is a 'proud *honourable* soul', but the father has a 'small, *mean* head'. This is the sustained contrast; the epithets are characteristic of the whole; and they represent half of Lawrence's feelings. But what is the other half? Which of these characters is given his real sympathy – the hard, self-righteous, aggressive, demanding mother who comes through to us, or the simple, direct, gentle, downright, fumbling, ruined father? There are two attitudes here. Lawrence (and Morel) loves his mother, but he also hates her for compelling his love; and he hates his father with the true Freudian jealousy, but he also loves him for what he is in himself, and he sympathizes more deeply with him because his wholeness has been destroyed by the mother's domination, just as his, Lawrence-Morel's, has been.

This is a psychological tension which disrupts the form of the novel and obscures its meaning, because neither the contradiction in style nor the confusion in point of view is made to right itself. Lawrence is merely repeating his emotions, and he avoids an austerer technical scrutiny of his material because it would compel him to master them. He would not let the artist be stronger than the man.

The result is that, at the same time that the book condemns the mother, it justifies her; at the same time that it shows Paul's failure, it offers rationalizations which place the failure elsewhere. The handling of the girl, Miriam, if viewed closely, is pathetic in what it signifies for Lawrence, both as a man and artist. For Miriam is made the mother's scape-goat, and in a different way from the way that she was in life. The central section of the novel is shot through with alternate statements as to the source of the difficulty: Paul is unable to love Miriam wholly, and Miriam can love only his spirit. The contradictions appear sometimes within single paragraphs, and the point of view is never adequately objectified and sustained to tell us which is true. The material is never seen as material; the writer is caught in it exactly as firmly as he was caught in his experience of it. 'That's how women are with me,' said Paul. 'They want me like mad, but they don't want to belong to me.' So he might have said, and believed it; but at the end of the novel, Lawrence is still saying that, and himself believing it.

For the full history of this technical failure, one must read *Sons and Lovers* carefully and then learn the history of the manuscript from the book called *D. H. Lawrence: A Personal Record*, by one E. T., who was Miriam in life. The basic situation is clear enough. The first theme – the crippling effects of the mother's love – is developed right through to the end; and then suddenly, in the last few sentences, turns on itself, and Paul gives himself to life, not death. But all the way through, the insidious rationalizations of the second theme have crept in to destroy the artistic coherence of the work. A 'split' would occur in Paul; but as the split is treated, it is superimposed upon rather than developed in support of the first theme. It is a rationalization made from it. If Miriam is made to insist on spiritual love, the meaning and the power of theme one are reduced; yet Paul's weakness is disguised. Lawrence could not separate the investigating analyst, who must be objective, from Lawrence, the subject of the book; and the sickness was not healed, the emotion not mastered, the novel not perfected. All this, and the character of a whole career, would have been altered if Lawrence had allowed his technique to discover the fullest meaning of his subject.

## NOTES

1. 'The best form is that which makes the most of its subject – there is no other definition of the meaning of form in fiction. The well-made book is the book in which the matter is all used up in the form, in which the form expresses all the matter.' Percy Lubbock, *The Craft of Fiction* (London and New York, 1921; Gloucester, Mass., 1947) p. 40.

2. See Eliot on 'Four Elizabethan Dramatists', in his *Selected Essays* (New York, 1932) p. 94.

# Dorothy Van Ghent
## ON *SONS AND LOVERS* (1953)

NOVELS, like other dramatic art, deal with conflicts of one kind or another – conflicts that are, in the work of the major novelists, drawn from life in the sense that they are representative of real problems in life; and the usual urgency in the novelist is to find the technical means which will afford an ideal resolution of the conflict and solution of the living problem – still 'ideal' even if tragic. Technique is his art itself, in its procedural aspect; and the validity of his solution of a problem is dependent upon the adequacy of his technique. The more complex and intransigent the problem, the more subtle his technical strategies will evidently need to be, if they are to be effective. The decade of World War I brought into full and terrible view the collapse of values that had prophetically haunted the minds of novelists as far back as Dostoevsky and Flaubert and Dickens, or even farther back, to Balzac and Stendhal. With that decade, and increasingly since, the problems of modern life have appeared intransigent indeed; and, in general, the growth of that intransigence has been reflected in an increasing concern with technique on the part of the artist. D. H. Lawrence's sensitivity to twentieth century chaos was peculiarly intense, and his passion for order was similarly intense; but this sensitivity and this passion did not lead him to concentrate on refinements and subtleties of novelistic technique in the direction laid out, for instance, by James and Conrad. Hence, as readers first approaching his work, almost inevitably we feel disappointment and even perhaps shock that writing so often 'loose' and repetitious and such unrestrained emotionalism over glandular matters should appear in the work of a novelist who is assumed to have an important place in the literary canon. 'There is no use', Francis Fergusson says, 'trying to appreciate

[Lawrence] solely as an artist; he was himself too often impatient of the demands of art, which seemed to him trivial compared with the quest he followed.'[1] And Stephen Spender phrases the problem of Lawrence in this way: what interested him 'was the tension between art and life, not the complete resolution of the problems of life within the illusion of art. . . . For him literature is a kind of pointer to what is outside literature. . . . This out-sideness of reality is for Lawrence the waters of baptism in which man can be reborn.'[2] We need to approach Lawrence with a good deal of humility about 'art' and a good deal of patience for the disappointments he frequently offers as an artist, for it is only thus that we shall be able to appreciate the innovations he actually made in the novel as well as the importance and pro-fundity of his vision of modern life.

*Sons and Lovers* appears to have the most conventional chronological organization; it is the kind of organization that a naïve autobiographical novelist would tend to use, with only the thinnest pretense at disguising the personally retrospective nature of the material. We start with the marriage of the parents and the birth of the children. We learn of the daily life of the family while the children are growing up, the work, the small joys, the parental strife. Certain well-defined emotional pressures become apparent: the children are alienated from their father, whose personality degenerates gradually as he feels his exclusion; the mother more and more completely dominates her sons' affections, aspirations, mental habits. Urged by her toward middle-class refinements, they enter white-collar jobs, thus making one more dissociation between themselves and their proletarian father. As they attempt to orient themselves toward biological adulthood, the old split in the family is manifested in a new form, as an internal schism in the characters of the sons; they cannot reconcile sexual choice with the idealism their mother has inculcated. This inner strain leads to the older son's death. The same motif is repeated in the case of Paul, the younger one. Paul's first girl, Miriam, is a cerebral type, and the mother senses in her an obvious rivalry for domination of Paul's sensibility. The mother is the stronger influence, and Paul withdraws from

Miriam; but with her own victory Mrs Morel begins to realize the discord she has produced in his character, and tries to release her hold on him by unconsciously seeking her own death. Paul finds another girl, Clara, but the damage is already too deeply designed, and at the time of his mother's death he voluntarily gives up Clara, knowing that there is but one direction he can take, and that is to go with his mother. At the end he is left emotionally derelict, with only the 'drift toward death'.

From this slight sketch, it is clear that the book is organized not merely on a chronological plan showing the habits and vicissitudes of a Nottinghamshire miner's family, but that it has a structure rigorously controlled by an idea: an idea of an organic disturbance in the relationships of men and women – a disturbance of sexual polarities that is first seen in the disaffection of mother and father, then in the mother's attempt to substitute her sons for her husband, finally in the sons' unsuccessful struggle to establish natural manhood. Lawrence's development of the idea has certain major implications: it implies that his characters have transgressed against the natural life-directed condition of the human animal – against the elementary biological rhythms he shares with the rest of biological nature; and it implies that this offense against life has been brought about by a failure to respect the complete and terminal individuality of persons – by a twisted desire to 'possess' other persons, as the mother tries to 'possess' her husband, then her sons, and as Miriam tries to 'possess' Paul. Lawrence saw this offense as a disease of modern life in all its manifestations, from sexual relationships to those broad social and political relationships that have changed people from individuals to anonymous economic properties or to military units or to ideological automatons.

The controlling idea is expressed in the various episodes – the narrative logic of the book. It is also expressed in imagery – the book's poetic logic. Perhaps in no other novelist do we find the image so largely replacing episode and discursive analysis, and taking over the expressive functions of these, as it does in Lawrence. The chief reason for the extraordinary predominance of the image as an absolute expressive medium in Lawrence lies in the character of the idea which is his subject. He must make us aware – sensitively aware, not merely conceptually aware – of the profound life force whose rhythms the natural creature obeys; and he must make us aware of the terminal individuality – the absolute 'otherness' or 'outsideness' – that is the natural form of things and of the uncorrupted person. We must be made aware of these through the *feelings* of his people, for only in feeling have the biological life force and the sense of identity – either the identity of self or of others – any immediacy of reality. He seeks the objective equivalent of feeling in the image. As Francis Fergusson says, Lawrence's imagination was so concrete that he seems not 'to distinguish between the reality and the metaphor or symbol which makes it plain to us'.[3] But the most valid symbols are the most concrete realities. Lawrence's great gift for the symbolic image was a function of his sensitivity to and passion for the meaning of real things – for the individual expression that real forms have. In other words, his gift for the image arose directly from his vision of life as infinitely creative of individual identities, each whole and separate and to be reverenced as such.

Let us examine the passage with which the first chapter of *Sons and Lovers* ends – where Mrs Morel, pregnant with Paul, wanders deliriously in the garden, shut out of the house by Morel in his drunkenness. Mrs Morel is literally a vessel of the life force that seems to thrust itself at her in nature from all sides, but she is also in rebellion against it and the perfume of the pollen-filled lilies makes her gasp with fear:

The moon was high and magnificent in the August night. Mrs Morel, seared with passion, shivered to find herself out there in a great white light, that fell cold on her, and gave a shock to her inflamed soul. She stood for a few moments helplessly staring at the glistening great rhubarb leaves near the door. Then she got the air into her breast. She walked down the garden path, trembling in every limb, while the child boiled within her. . . .
She hurried out of the side garden to the front, where she could stand as if in an immense gulf of white light, the moon streaming high in face of her, the moonlight standing up from

the hills in front, and filling the valley where the Bottoms crouched, almost blindingly. There, panting and half weeping in reaction from the stress, she murmured to herself over and over again: 'The nuisance! the nuisance!'

She became aware of something about her. With an effort she roused herself to see what it was that penetrated her consciousness. The tall white lilies were reeling in the moonlight, and the air was charged with their perfume, as with a presence. Mrs Morel gasped slightly in fear. She touched the big, pallid flowers on their petals, then shivered. They seemed to be stretching in the moonlight. She put her hand into one white bin: the gold scarcely showed on her fingers by moonlight. She bent down to look at the binful of yellow pollen; but it only appeared dusky. Then she drank a deep draught of the scent. It almost made her dizzy.

Mrs Morel leaned on the garden gate, looking out, and she lost herself awhile. She did not know what she thought. Except for a slight feeling of sickness, and her consciousness in the child, herself melted out like scent into the shiny, pale air. (ch. 1)

She finally arouses Morel from his drunken sleep and he lets her in. Unfastening her brooch at the bedroom mirror, she sees that her face is smeared with the yellow dust of the lilies.

The imagery of the streaming moonlight is that of a vast torrential force, 'magnificent' and inhuman, and it equates not only with that phallic power of which Mrs Morel is the rebellious vessel but with the greater and universal demiurge that was anciently called Eros – the power springing in plants and hurling the planets, giving the 'glistening great rhubarb leaves' their fierce identity, fecundating and stretching the lilies. The smear of yellow pollen on Mrs Morel's face is a grossly humorous irony. This passage is a typifying instance of the spontaneous identification Lawrence constantly found between image and meaning, between real things and what they symbolize.

Our particular culture has evolved deep prohibitions against the expression, or even the subjective acknowledgment of the kind of phallic reality with which Lawrence was concerned – and with which ancient religions were also concerned. Certainly one factor in the uneasiness that Lawrence frequently causes us is the factor of those cultural prohibitions. But these prohibitions themselves Lawrence saw as disease symptoms, though the disease was far more extensive and radical than a taboo on the phallus. It was a spiritual disease that broke down the sense of identity, of 'separate selfhood', while at the same time it broke down the sense of rhythm with universal nature. Paul Morel, working his fairly unconscious, adolescent, sexual way toward Miriam, finds that rhythm and that selfhood in the spatial proportions of a wren's nest in a hedge:

He crouched down and carefully put his finger through the thorns into the round door of the nest.

'It's almost as if you were feeling inside the live body of the bird,' he said, 'it's so warm. They say a bird makes its nest round like a cup with pressing its breast on it. Then how did it make the ceiling round, I wonder?' (ch. VII)

When Paul takes his first country walk with Clara and Miriam, the appearance of a red stallion in the woods vividly realizes in unforced symbolic dimension the power which will drive Paul from Miriam to Clara, while the image also realizes the great horse itself in its unique and mysterious identity:

As they were going beside the brook, on the Willey Water side, looking through the brake at the edge of the wood, where pink campions glowed under a few sunbeams, they saw, beyond the tree-trunks and the thin hazel bushes, a man leading a great bay horse through the gullies. The big red beast seemed to dance romantically through that dimness of green hazel drift, away there where the air was shadowy, as if it were in the past, among the fading bluebells that might have bloomed for Deirdre. . . .

The great horse breathed heavily, shifting round its red flanks, and looking suspiciously with its wonderful big eyes upwards from under its lowered head and falling mane. (ch. IX)

A simple descriptive passage like the following, showing a hen pecking at a girl's hand, conveys the animal dynamics that is the urgent phase of the phallic power working in the boy and the girl, but its spontaneous symbolism of a larger reality is due to its faithfulness to the way a hen does peck and the feeling of the pecking – due, that is, to the actuality or 'identity' of the small, homely circumstance itself:

As he went round the back, he saw Miriam kneeling in front of the hencoop, some maize in her hand, biting her lip, and crouching in an intense attitude. The hen was eyeing her wickedly. Very gingerly she put forward her hand. The hen bobbed for her. She drew back quickly with a cry, half of fear, half of chagrin.

'It won't hurt you,' said Paul.

She flushed crimson and started up.

'I only wanted to try,' she said in a low voice.

'See, it doesn't hurt,' he said, and, putting only two corns in his palm, he let the hen peck, peck, peck at his bare hand. 'It only makes you laugh,' he said.

She put her hand forward, and dragged it away, tried again, and started back with a cry. He frowned.

'Why, I'd let her take corn from my face,' said Paul, 'only she bumps a bit. She's ever so neat. If she wasn't, look how much ground she'd peck up every day.'

He waited grimly, and watched. At last Miriam let the bird peck from her hand. She gave a little cry – fear, and pain because of fear – rather pathetic. But she had done it, and she did it again.

'There, you see,' said the boy. 'It doesn't hurt, does it?' (ch. vi)

There is more terse and obvious symbolism, of the kind typical in Lawrence, in that sequence where Clara's red carnations splatter their petals over her clothes and on the ground where she and Paul first make love, but we acquire the best and the controlling sense of Lawrence's gift for the image, as dramatic and thematic expression, in those passages where his urgency is to see *things* and to see them clearly and completely in their most individualizing traits, for the character of his vision is such that, in truly seeing them as they are, he sees through them to what they mean.

We frequently notice the differentiating significance of a writer's treatment of nature – that is, of that part of 'nature' which is constituted by earth and air and water and the non-human creatures; and we find that attitudes toward nature are deeply associated with attitudes toward human 'good', human destiny, human happiness, human salvation, the characteristic problems of being human. One might cite, for instance, in *Tom Jones*, Fielding's highly stylized treatment of outdoor nature (as in the passage in which Tom dreams of Sophia beside the brook, and Mollie Seagrim approaches): here nature has only generalized attributes for whose description and understanding certain epithets in common educated currency are completely adequate – brooks murmur, breezes whisper, birds trill; nature is really a linguistic construction, and this rationalization of nature is appropriate in Fielding's universe since everything there exists ideally as an object of *ratio*, of reasoning intelligence. We notice in Jane Austen's *Pride and Prejudice* (in the description of Darcy's estate, for example) that outdoor nature again has importance only as it serves to express rational and social character – wherefore again the generalized epithet that represents nature as either the servant of intelligence or the space where intelligence operates. In George Eliot's *Adam Bede*, where there is relatively a great deal of 'outdoors', nature is man's plowfield, the acre in which he finds social and ethical expression through work; this is only a different variety of the conception of nature as significant by virtue of what man's intelligential and social character makes of it for his ends.

With Emily Brontë, we come nearer to Lawrence, though not very near. In *Wuthering Heights*, nature's importance is due not to its yielding itself up to domestication in man's reason, or offering itself as an instrument by which he expresses his conscience before God or society, but to its fiercely unregenerate difference from all that civilized man is – a difference that it constantly forces on perception by animal-like attacks on and disruptions of human order. In Hardy, nature is also a daemonic entity in its own right, and not only unrationalizable but specifically hostile to the human reason. It is worth noting that, among all English novelists, Hardy and Lawrence have the most faithful touch for the things of nature and the greatest evocative genius in bringing them before the imagination. But there are certain definitive differences of attitude. Both Emily Brontë's and Hardy's worlds are dual, and there is no way of bringing the oppositions of the dualism together: on the one side of the cleavage are those attributes of man that we call 'human', his reason, his ethical sensibility; and on the other side is 'nature' –

the elements and the creatures and man's own instinctive life
that he shares with the nonhuman creatures. The opposition is
resolved only by destruction of the 'human': a destruction that is
in Emily Brontë profoundly attractive, in Hardy tragic. But
Lawrence's world is multiple rather than dual. Everything in
it is a separate and individual 'other', every person, every creature,
every object (like the madonna lilies, the rhubarb plants, the
wren's nest, the stallion); and there is a creative relationship
between people and between people and things so long as this
'otherness' is acknowledged. When it is denied – and it is denied
when man tries to rationalize nature and society, or when he
presumptuously assumes the things of nature to be merely instruments for the expression of himself, or when he attempts to
exercise personal possessorship over people – then he destroys
his own selfhood and exerts a destructive influence all about him.

In *Sons and Lovers*, only in Morel himself, brutalized and
spiritually maimed as he is, does the germ of selfhood remain
intact; and – this is the correlative proposition in Lawrence – in
him only does the biological life force have simple, unequivocal
assertion. Morel wants to live, by hook or crook, while his sons
want to die. To live is to obey a rhythm involving more than
conscious attitudes and involving more than human beings –
involving all nature; a rhythm indifferent to the greediness of
reason, indifferent to idiosyncrasies of culture and idealism. The
image associated with Morel is that of the coalpits, where he
descends daily and from which he ascends at night blackened and
tired. It is a symbol of rhythmic descent and ascent, like a sexual
rhythm, or like the rhythm of sleep and awaking or of death and
life. True, the work in the coalpits reverses the natural use of the
hours of light and dark and is an economic distortion of that
rhythm in nature – and Morel and the other colliers bear the
spiritual traumata of that distortion; for Lawrence is dealing
with the real environment of modern men, in its complexity and
injuriousness. Nevertheless, the work at the pits is still symbolic
of the greater rhythm governing life and obedience to which is
salvation. Throughout the book, the coalpits are always at the
horizon:

On the fallow land the young wheat shone silkily. Minton pit waved its plumes of white steam, coughed, and rattled hoarsely.
'Now look at that!' said Mrs Morel. Mother and son stood on the road to watch. Along the ridge of the great pit-hill crawled a little group in silhouette against the sky, a horse, a small truck, and a man. They climbed the incline against the heavens. At the end the man tipped the waggon. There was an undue rattle as the waste fell down the sheer slope of the enormous bank. . . .
'Look how it heaps together,' [Paul says of the pit] 'like something alive almost – a big creature that you don't know. . . . And all the trucks standing waiting, like a string of beasts to be fed. . . . I like the feel of *men* on things, while they're alive. There's a feel of men about trucks, because they've been handled with men's hands, all of them.' (ch. VI)

Paul associates the pits not only with virility but with being alive. The trucks themselves become alive because they have been handled by men. The symbolism of the pits is identical with that of Morel, the father, the irrational life principle that is unequally embattled against the death principle in the mother, the rational and idealizing principle working rhythmlessly, greedily, presumptuously, and possessively.

The sons' attitude toward the father is ambivalent, weighted toward hate because the superior cultural equipment of the mother shows his crudeness in relief; but again and again bits of homely characterization of Morel show that the children – and even the mother herself – sense, however uncomfortably, the attractiveness of his simple masculine integrity. He has, uninjurable, what the mother's possessiveness has injured in the sons:

'Shut that doo-er!' bawled Morel furiously.
Annie banged it behind her, and was gone.
'If tha oppens it again while I'm weshin' me, I'll ma'e thy jaw rattle,' he threatened from the midst of his soapsuds. Paul and the mother frowned to hear him.
Presently he came running out of the scullery, with the soapy water dripping from him, dithering with cold.
'Oh, my sirs!' he said. 'Wheer's my towel?'
It was hung on a chair to warm before the fire, otherwise he

would have bullied and blustered. He squatted on his heels before the hot baking-fire to dry himself.

'F-ff-f!' he went, pretending to shudder with cold.

'Goodness, man, don't be such a kid!' said Mrs Morel. 'It's *not* cold.'

'Thee strip thysen stark nak'd to wesh thy flesh i' that scullery,' said the miner, as he rubbed his hair; 'nowt b'r a ice-'ouse!'

'And I shouldn't make that fuss,' replied this wife.

'No, tha'd drop down stiff, as dead as a door-knob, wi' thy nesh sides.'

'Why is a door-knob deader than anything else?' asked Paul, curious.

'Eh, I dunno; that's what they say,' replied his father. 'But there's that much draught i' yon scullery, as it blows through your ribs like through a five-barred gate.'

'It would have some difficulty in blowing through yours,' said Mrs Morel.

Morel looked down ruefully at his sides.

'Me!' he exclaimed. 'I'm nowt b'r a skinned rabbit. My bones fair juts out on me.'

'I should like to know where,' retorted his wife.

'Iv-ry-wheer! I'm nobbut a sack o' faggots.'

Mrs Morel laughed. He had still a wonderfully young body, muscular, without any fat. His skin was smooth and clear. It might have been the body of a man of twenty-eight, except that there were, perhaps, too many blue scars, like tattoo-marks, where the coal-dust remained under the skin, and that his chest was too hairy. But he put his hands on his sides ruefully. It was his fixed belief that, because he did not get fat, he was as thin as a starved rat.

Paul looked at his father's thick, brownish hands all scarred, with broken nails, rubbing the fine smoothness of his sides, and the incongruity struck him. It seemed strange they were the same flesh. (ch. VIII)

Morel talks the dialect that is the speech of physical tenderness in Lawrence's books.[4] It is to the dialect of his father that Paul reverts when he is tussling with Beatrice in adolescent erotic play (letting the mother's bread burn, that he should have been watching), and that Arthur, the only one of the sons whom the

mother has not corrupted, uses in his love-making, and that Paul
uses again when he makes love to Clara, the uncomplex woman
who is able for a while to give him his sexual manhood and his
'separate selfhood'. The sons never use the dialect with their
mother, and Paul never uses it with Miriam. It is the speech used
by Mellors in *Lady Chatterley's Lover*; and, significantly perhaps,
Mellors' name is an anagram on the name Morel.

Some of the best moments in the children's life are associated
with the father, when Morel has his 'good' periods and enters
again into the intimate activity of the family – and some of the
best, most simply objective writing in the book communicates
these moments, as for instance the passage in chapter IV where
Morel is engaged in making fuses:

. . . Morel fetched a sheaf of long sound wheat-straws from the
attic. These he cleaned with his hand, till each one gleamed like
a stalk of gold, after which he cut the straws into lengths of about
six inches, leaving, if he could, a notch at the bottom of each piece.
He always had a beautifully sharp knife that could cut a straw
clean without hurting it. Then he set in the middle of the table
a heap of gun-powder, a little pile of black grains upon the
white-scrubbed board. He made and trimmed the straws while
Paul and Annie filled and plugged them. Paul loved to see the
black grains trickle down a crack in his palm into the mouth of
the straw, peppering jollily downwards till the straw was full.
Then he bunged up the mouth with a bit of soap – which he got
on his thumb-nail from a pat in a saucer – and the straw was
finished.

There is a purity of realization in this very simple kind of exposition that, on the face of it, resists associating itself with any
*symbolic* function – if we tend to think of a 'symbol' as splitting
itself apart into a thing and a meaning, with a mental arrow con-
necting the two. The best in Lawrence carries the authenticity
of a faithfully observed, concrete actuality that refuses to be
split; its symbolism is a radiation that leaves it intact in itself.
So, in the passage above, the scene is intact as homely realism,
but it radiates Lawrence's controlling sense of the characterful
integrity of objects – the clean wheat straws, the whitely scrubbed

table, the black grains peppering down a crack in the child's palm, the bung of soap on a thumbnail – and that integrity is here associated with the man Morel and his own integrity of warm and absolute maleness. Thus it is another representation of the creative life force witnessed in the independent objectivity of things that are wholly concrete and wholly themselves.

The human attempt to distort and corrupt that selfhood is reflected in Miriam's attitude toward flowers:

Round the wild, tussocky lawn at the back of the house was a thorn hedge, under which daffodils were craning forward from among their sheaves of grey-green blades. The cheeks of the flowers were greenish with cold. But still some had burst, and their gold ruffled and glowed. Miriam went on her knees before one cluster, took a wild-looking daffodil between her hands, turned up its face of gold to her, and bowed down, caressing it with her mouth and cheeks and brow. He stood aside, with his hands in his pockets, watching her. One after another she turned up to him the faces of the yellow, bursten flowers appealingly, fondling them lavishly all the while. . . .

'Why must you always be fondling things!' he said irritably. . . . 'Can you never like things without clutching them as if you wanted to pull the heart out of them? . . . You're always begging things to love you. . . . Even the flowers, you have to fawn on them –'

Rhythmically, Miriam was swaying and stroking the flower with her mouth. . . .

'You don't want to love – your eternal and abnormal craving is to be loved. You aren't positive, you're negative. You absorb, absorb, as if you must fill yourself up with love, because you've got a shortage somewhere.' (ch. IX)

The relationship of the girl to the flowers is that of a blasphemous possessorship which denies the separateness of living entities – the craving to break down boundaries between thing and thing, that is seen also in Miriam's relationship with Paul, whom she cannot love without trying to absorb him. In contrast, there is the flower imagery in chapter XI, where Paul goes out into the night and the garden in a moment of emotional struggle:

It grew late. Through the open door, stealthily, came the scent of madonna lilies, almost as if it were prowling abroad. Suddenly he got up and went out of doors.

The beauty of the night made him want to shout. A half-moon, dusky gold, was sinking behind the black sycamore at the end of the garden, making the sky dull purple with its glow. Nearer, a dim white fence of lilies went across the garden, and the air all round seemed to stir with scent, as if it were alive. He went across the bed of pinks, whose keen perfume came sharply across the rocking, heavy scent of the lilies, and stood alongside the white barrier of flowers. They flagged all loose, as if they were panting. The scent made him drunk. He went down to the field to watch the moon sink under.

A corncrake in the hay-close called insistently. The moon slid quite quickly downwards, growing more flushed. Behind him the great flowers leaned as if they were calling. And then, like a shock, he caught another perfume, something raw and coarse. Hunting round, he found the purple iris, touched their fleshy throats and their dark, grasping hands. At any rate, he had found something. They stood stiff in the darkness. Their scent was brutal. The moon was melting down upon the crest of the hill. It was gone; all was dark. The corncrake called still.

The flowers here have a fierce 'thereness' or 'otherness' establishing them as existences in their own right – as separate, strange selves – and the demiurgic Eros is rudely insistent in their scent. Paul's perception of that independent life puts him into relation with himself, and the moment of catalytic action is marked by the brief sentence: 'At any rate, he had found something.' The 'something' that he finds is simply the iris, dark, fleshy, mysterious, alien. He goes back into the house and tells his mother that he has decided to break off with Miriam.

Darkness – as the darkness of this night in the garden – has in Lawrence a special symbolic potency. It is a natural and universal symbol, but it offers itself with special richness to Lawrence because of the character of his governing vision. Darkness is half of the rhythm of the day, the darkness of unconsciousness is half of the rhythm of the mind, and the darkness of death is half of the rhythm of life. Denial of this phase of the universal tide is the great sin, the sin committed by modern economy and modern rationalism. In acceptance of the dark, man is renewed to himself – and to light, to consciousness, to reason, to brotherhood. But by refusal to accept that half of the rhythm, he becomes impotent, his reason becomes destructive, and he loses the sense of the independence of others which is essential to brotherhood. In chapter XIII of *Sons and Lovers* there is a passage that realizes something of what we have been saying. It occurs just after Paul has made love to Clara in a field:

All the while the peewits were screaming in the field. When he came to, he wondered what was near his eyes, curving and strong with life in the dark, and what voice it was speaking. Then he realized it was the grass, and the peewit was calling. The warmth was Clara's breathing heaving. He lifted his head, and looked into her eyes. They were dark and shining and strange, life wild at the source staring into his life, stranger to him, yet meeting him; and he put his face down on her throat, afraid. What was she? A strong, strange, wild life, that breathed with his in the darkness through this hour. It was all so much bigger than themselves that he was hushed. They had met, and included in their meeting the thrust of the manifold grass-stems, the cry of the peewit, the wheel of the stars. . . .

. . . after such an evening they both were very still. . . . They felt small, half afraid, childish, and wondering, like Adam and Eve when they lost their innocence and realized the magnificence of the power which drove them out of Paradise and across the great night and the great day of humanity. It was for each of them an initiation. . . . To know their own nothingness, to know the tremendous living flood which carried them always, gave them rest within themselves. If so great a magnificent power could overwhelm them, identify them altogether with itself, so that they knew they were only grains in the tremendous heave that lifted every grass-blade its little height, and every tree, and living thing, then why fret about themselves? They could let themselves be carried by life, and they felt a sort of peace each in the other. There was a verification which they had had together. Nothing could nullify it, nothing could take it away; it was almost their belief in life.

But then we are told that 'Clara was not satisfied. . . . She thought it was he whom she wanted. . . . She had not got him; she was not satisfied.' This is the impulse toward personal possessorship that constantly confuses and distorts human relationships in Lawrence's books; it is a denial of the otherness of people, and a denial, really, of the great inhuman life force, the primal 'otherness' through which people have their independent definition as well as their creative community. Paul had felt that 'his experience had been impersonal, and not Clara'; and he had wanted the same impersonality in Clara, an impersonality consonant with that of the manifold grass stems and the peewits' calling, the wheel of the stars. André Malraux, in his preface to the French translation of *Lady Chatterley's Lover*, says that this 'couple-advocate' Lawrence, is concerned not with his own individuality or that of his mate, but with 'being': 'Lawrence has no wish to be either happy or great,' Malraux says; 'he is only concerned with being.'[5] The concern with being, with simple being-a-self (as distinguished from imposing the ego or abdicating selfhood in the mass), can be understood only in the context of twentieth century man's resignation to herd ideologies, herd recreations, herd rationalizations. Lawrence's missionary and prophetic impulse, like Dostoevsky's, was to combat the excesses of rationalism and individualism, excesses that have led – paradoxically enough – to the release of monstrously destructive irrationals and to the impotence of the individual. He wanted to bring man's self-definition and creativity back into existence through recognition of and vital relationship with the rhythms that men share with the nonhuman world; for he thought that thus men could find not only the selves that they had denied, but also the brotherhood they had lost.

The darkness of the phallic consciousness is the correlative of a passionate life assertion, strong as the thrust of the grass stems in the field where Paul and Clara make love, and as the dynamics of the wheeling stars. 'In the lowest trough of the night' there is always 'a flare of the pit.' A pillar of cloud by day, the pit is a pillar of fire by night: and the Lord is at the pit top. As a descent of darkness and an ascent of flame is associated with the secret, essential, scatheless maleness of the father, so also the passionate self-forgetful play of the children is associated with a fiery light in the night – an isolated lamp-post, a blood-red moon, and behind, 'the great scoop of darkness, as if all the night were there'. It is this understanding of the symbolism of darkness in Lawrence that gives tragic dignity to such a scene as that of the bringing home of William's coffin through the darkness of the night:

Morel and Paul went, with a candle, into the parlour. There was no gas there. The father unscrewed the top of the big mahogany oval table, and cleared the middle of the room; then he arranged six chairs opposite each other, so that the coffin could stand on their beds.

'You niver seed such a length as he is!' said the miner, and watching anxiously as he worked.

Paul went to the bay window and looked out. The ash-tree stood monstrous and black in front of the wide darkness. It was a faintly luminous night. Paul went back to his mother.

At ten o'clock Morel called:

'He's here!'

Everyone started. There was a noise of unbarring and unlocking the front door, which opened straight from the night into the room.

'Bring another candle,' called Morel. . . .

There was the noise of wheels. Outside in the darkness of the street below Paul could see horses and a black vehicle, one lamp, and a few pale faces; then some men, miners, all in their shirt-sleeves, seemed to struggle in the obscurity. Presently two men appeared, bowed beneath a great weight. It was Morel and his neighbour.

'Steady!' called Morel, out of breath.

He and his fellow mounted the steep garden step, heaved into the candlelight with their gleaming coffin-end. Limbs of other men were seen struggling behind. Morel and Burns, in front, staggered; the great dark weight swayed.

'Steady, steady!' cried Morel, as if in pain. . . .

The coffin swayed, the men began to mount the three steps with their load. Annie's candle flickered, and she whimpered as the first men appeared, and the limbs and bowed heads of six men struggled to climb into the room, bearing the coffin that rode like sorrow on their living flesh. (ch. VI)

Here the darkness appears in another indivisible aspect of its mystery – as the darkness of death. Perhaps no other modern writer besides Rilke and Mann has tried so sincerely to bring death into relationship with life as Lawrence did, and each under the assumption that life, to know itself creatively, must know its relationship with death; a relationship which the ethos of some hundred and fifty years of rationalism and industrialism and 'progress' have striven to exorcise, and by that perversion brought men to an abject worship of death and to holocausts such as that of Hiroshima. *Sons and Lovers* ends with Paul a derelict in the 'drift toward death', which Lawrence thought of as the disease syndrome of his time and of Europe. But the death drift, the death worship, is for Lawrence a hideous distortion of the relationship of death to life. In the scene in which William's coffin is brought home, the front door 'opened straight from the night into the room'. So, in their rhythmic proportions, life and death open straight into each other, as do the light of consciousness and the darkness of the unconscious, and the usurpation of either one is a perversion of the other. Stephen Spender calls Lawrence 'the most hopeful modern writer'. His 'dark gods', Spender says,

. . . are symbols of an inescapable mystery: the point of comprehension where the senses are aware of an otherness in objects which extends beyond the senses, and the possibility of a relationship between the human individual and the forces outside himself, which is capable of creating in him a new state of mind. Lawrence is the most hopeful modern writer, because he looks beyond the human to the nonhuman, which can be discovered within the human.[6]

## NOTES

1. Fergusson, 'D. H. Lawrence's Sensibility', in *Critiques and Essays in Modern Fiction*, ed. John W. Aldridge (New York, 1952) p. 328.
2. Spender, 'The Life of Literature', in *Partisan Review*, Dec. 1948.
3. Fergusson, op. cit., p. 335.
4. This observation is made by Diana Trilling in her Introduction to *The Portable D. H. Lawrence* (New York, 1947).
5. In *Criterion*, XII xlvii (1932–3) 217.
6. Spender, op. cit.

*Seymour Betsky*

# RHYTHM AND THEME: D. H. LAWRENCE'S *SONS AND LOVERS* (1953)

I

*Sons and Lovers* moves along a structural pattern determined by the nature of its human relationships. A wave-rhythm distinguishes, in beat and counterbeat, the major involvements of the characters: those of Walter and Gertrude Morel, Paul and his mother, Paul and Miriam, and Paul and Clara. In each of these relationships, separate episodes focus – in dramatically enacted dialogue, description, and action – aspects of each character-interconnection. Each event is a successive wave, and the movement of the relationship is the full tide which is its consummation. After that consummation, there are wave-like returns to the achieved tension in that relationship, but now each wave shows a diminishing strength and intensity. The reader of *Sons and Lovers* soon comes to anticipate the rhythmic returns and finds himself attuned to the Lawrencean mode. He doesn't ask for the conventional climactic development.

This impression strikes the reader, however indirectly, in Lawrence's own account of that novel. On its completion in 1912, he wrote the well-known letter to his editor, Edward Garnett, which said in part:

It follows this idea: a woman of character and refinement goes into the lower class, and has no satisfaction in her own life. She has had a passion for her husband, so the children are born of passion, and have heaps of vitality. But as her sons grow up she selects them as lovers – first the eldest, then the second. These sons are *urged* into life by their reciprocal love of their mother – urged on and on. But when they come to manhood, they can't love, because their mother is the strongest power in their lives, and holds them.... As soon as the young men come into contact with women, there's a split. William gives his sex to a fribble, and his mother holds his soul. But the split kills him, because he doesn't know where he is. The next son gets a woman who fights for his soul – fights his mother. The son loves the mother – all the sons hate and are jealous of the father. The battle goes on between the mother and the girl, with the son as object. The mother gradually proves stronger, because of the tie of blood. The son decides to leave his soul in his mother's hands, and, like his elder brother, go for passion. He gets passion. Then the split begins to tell again. But, almost unconsciously, the mother realizes what is the matter and begins to die. The son casts off his mistress, attends to his mother dying. He is left in the end naked of everything, with the drift towards death.*

Lawrence's 'explanation' is only a temporary convenience, the novelist assuring the reader that the reader has taken the novel thematically as it was largely intended. It omits perforce the detail, the subtlety, and the complexity of his own exploration. It gives no sense of the way in which the novel slowly tortures itself into shape through alternate expansion and economy, working with experiences selected from closest autobiography, while remaining in the end a successful novel, not a case history. Principally, however, Lawrence's letter fails sufficiently to convey the impression of his novel's rhythmic insistence. The novel actually creates the theme, beat by rhythmic beat. Paul's relation to his mother reaches its decisive point when William dies and he takes William's place at the center of his mother's life. Once Paul's interests take him outside the home, the strength, in turn, of that relationship diminishes, though there is no decisive falling off.

* 'Never trust the author, trust the tale.' Lawrence's own words become irony in reverse. He misleads. To say that the 'mother proves stronger because of the tie of blood' is to call attention away from the manner in which the novel itself builds up cumulatively the more formidable impression of her strength of character. The 'tie of blood' is by far the subordinate impression. If we 'trust the tale' and not Lawrence, we squirm at the oversimplification of: 'The son decides to leave his soul in his mother's hands, and, like his elder brother, go for passion.' Further, Lawrence positively errs. It is clear that the 'drift towards death' contradicts the ending of the novel.

The relationship of Gertrude and Walter Morel has reached its consummation before the main action of the novel begins. After that, explosive quarrels in succession mark the decline. The passional sexual attraction of Paul and Clara reaches its crest quickly, its disintegration quickly. And the defeat of Miriam comes at a relatively early stage. Even though there is return in almost nagging repetition in much of the novel that follows, the note of defeat in the coda predominates.

II

The reader must go further than Lawrence's thematic account, assenting to its barest outline only. Actually, the unconscious intention of the novel presses forward more urgently as the satisfactory thematic account. *Sons and Lovers*, is, in fact, an *apologia*, a self-purgation that attempts to set down, with as much detail and detachment as this intimate biography will permit, a major experience in Lawrence's own life. As such, it compels the finest discrimination: how much of the novel is successfully realized? How much remains unresolved biography?

Clearly, those parts of the novel having to do with Gertrude Morel are its strength, this in spite of a degree of idealization. Even those scenes where she figures only indirectly gain in clarity as she moves forcibly in the background. The detailed, dimensional sense of the living force that is Gertrude Morel asserts itself only after countless little scenes with her husband, her sons, and her neighbors. The relationship with her husband is characterized first by violence, then by a considerable abatement of established hostility once the children are grown. Her relationship with William never moves to the center, partly because Lawrence for his own novelist's reasons decides against it, partly because William leaves home comparatively early in life. The rhythmic pattern of the mother's relationship with Paul is strongest after William's death. It suffers a displacement once Miriam enters Paul's life seriously. Even the descents into explicitness that, in their generalizing insistence, become a vice of style in the 'Miriam' episodes (and in the later novels), come with an economic terseness, in the 'Gertrude Morel' episodes, *after* the successfully presented scene.

Lawrence shows also a sure command of the resources of the language, the vigorous, idiomatic folk language that has behind it a rich communal experience. His most successful scenes follow precisely the movement and dialect of speech: compactly, where the scene carries its own weight; in leisurely fashion, where thematic development demands more space. The reader may find any number of effective scenes. The descriptions of the death of William and of the painful death of Gertrude Morel are perhaps the most moving, but there are easily a dozen others, all centering around Gertrude Morel, that come vividly to mind. While there are other fine scenes where Mrs Morel does not figure, these do not have the force, the bite, and the clarity of the events in which she is prime mover, or one of the principal agents.

The catharsis that Lawrence achieves from the outset in that part of the novel given over to Gertrude Morel (and, less importantly, to Clara) figures, then, for the reader as 'realization' – as though Lawrence were following the inevitable sequence of events as the pressure of theme dictated. It is inevitable that a mother, especially a woman as gifted for living as Mrs Morel, should not wish to see her sons wasted. There is, in fact, the poignancy of another dimension in Lawrence, not to be found in either Joyce or Eliot, that comes from the closeness of Mrs Morel's relationship with her sons and her touching concern that each discover some satisfaction in vocation and marriage. It is inevitable, too, that she should want her children to move out of the mining community – as each does on maturity. Most of all, we follow the disaster of her marriage in a way that emphasizes not the fault of the wife or the husband so much as the inevitability: 'The pity was, she was too much his opposite. She could not be content with the little he might be; she would have him the much that he ought to be. So, in seeking to make him nobler than he could be, she destroyed him.' Yet the disintegration was unavoidable: 'Sometimes, when she wearied of love-talk, she tried to open her heart seriously to him. She saw him listen deferentially, but without understanding. This killed her efforts at a finer intimacy, and she had flashes of fear.'

The surest touches in the novel, however, are not generalizations of this order. They are applied implicitly. When we reread the novel for this purpose, we are surprised to perceive, for example, the innumerable, careful strokes that pile up the impression of Walter Morel. We remember most vividly, perhaps, his drunkenness and savagery, the deceit before the marriage that made Gertrude Coppard believe him to be a man of some property and money, his unmanly self-pity when ill or injured, his lack of understanding of anything in the children beyond the possibility of their adaptability to a miner's life, and the core of superstitious ignorance in the man. But there are also his folk mimicry, his skill with his hands, his tenderness to wife and children in the intervals of peace within the family, his love of song and of dance, and his animal vigor. Although shiftless and careless part of the time, he works hard for his family in a dangerous occupation. Nor is there any pretentiousness about him; his working-class pride wins respect. And there is a strong sense of pathos attaching to a man defeated by a woman stronger and more intelligent.

An even greater richness of detail creates the formidable complexity that is Morel's wife. It is true that she uses her children as instruments of her will, to enable them to realize fulfillment where she knew only bitter frustration. By thrusting 'success' imperiously upon her sons for her sake, she imposes on them an almost ineradicable sense of guilt in their progress through a difficult world. Moreover, by sharing intimately their developing ideas, their crises, their deepest affections and hatreds at the most impressionable times of their lives, she possesses them as individuals and defeats them, almost, as lovers. She enjoys the enormous advantage of enveloping her children as the family meets poverty, suffering, and death. Even her sense of 'play' with her children is so delicate that the sons find it hard to duplicate in their adult relationships with other women.

Although Freud cannot be considered a significant influence, the implicit Freudian pattern in *Sons and Lovers* is developed with an insistence that is surely more daring for its time than *Lady Chatterley's Lover* was (in its very different way) for its time. Lawrence here is scrupulous, is honest: 'Being the sons of mothers whose husbands had blundered rather brutally through their feminine sanctities, they were themselves too diffident and shy. They could easier deny themselves than incur any reproach from a woman; for a woman was like their mother. They preferred themselves to suffer the misery of celibacy, rather than risk the other person.' There is the scene in which Paul has allowed the bread to burn while he is giving French lessons to Miriam. His mother returns, and mother and son have what amounts to a lover's quarrel, to the point where Paul, to reassure his mother (who is made ill by the novelist, perhaps to gloss over the painful immediacy of mother-son intimacy), 'stroked his mother's hair, and his mouth was on her throat'. The father enters, brutally drunk, and he has a jealous wrangle with his son. It is the one scene involving Mrs Morel that is too uncomfortably direct for the novel, and the chapter ends with: 'Everybody tried to forget the scene' – as though Lawrence himself wished to thrust it out of consciousness. There are instances, however, where the objectification is more successful: the scene where Walter and Gertrude Morel have one of their bitterest conflicts, symbolically while Paul is still an unborn child, so that when Mrs Morel goes outside to calm herself, the unborn baby 'boils inside her'. Again, there is the controlled scene in which the anxieties of the mother waiting for the return of her husband, probably drunk and violent, are transferred to Paul.

Above all, Gertrude Morel is a powerful woman in her own right. She is well read, quick in perceptions, and she shows a native common sense of a high order. From 'a good old burgher family, famous independents who had fought with Colonel Hutchinson', but impoverished in later generations, she is transplanted into a mining community some time after she leaves her schoolteacher's job. Without a trace of self-pity, she adapts herself to the hard life of a miner's wife. She does her own cooking, baking, and sewing, and lives restricted by the tough frugalities of a miner's life. Pride in her background acts as a stiff barrier between her and the community, but she adapts herself to that community with intelligence. It is she who *makes* the home of which Paul is proud:

There was about it now, he thought, a certain distinction. The chairs were only wooden, and the sofa was old. But the hearthrug and cushions were cosy; the pictures were prints in good taste; there was simplicity in everything, and plenty of books. He was never ashamed in the least of his home, nor was Miriam of hers, because both were what they should be, and warm. And then he was proud of the table; the china was pretty, the cloth was fine. It did not matter that the spoons were not silver nor the knives ivory-handled; everything looked nice. Mrs Morel managed wonderfully while her children were growing up, so that nothing was out of place. (ch. VIII)

Her religion is practical and nonrepressive. It is the kind of Puritanism that accepts a difficult lot without complaint, yet is touched with an aliveness, a joy in living. Gertrude Morel demonstrates an admirable impersonality in the face of a disastrous marriage, poverty, and death – the impersonality of the biblical chant, for example, when William's coffin is brought into the room. Paul inherits that attitude: 'What happened happened, and it was no good kicking against the pricks.' One saw oneself with clarity; made the most of it; was honest and fair in business dealings and personal relationships; and never whined. The absence of any trace of self-commiseration in Paul, delicate in health from the outset, has a Keatsian quality. Mrs Morel has, moreover, a sense of fun, of holiday, and some of the best parts of the book describe her excursions with Paul. He takes from her his sensitivity to the natural world, his love of flower-gifts, and to clothes in good taste. Above all, the sensuous fulfillment of the early months of her marriage operates as a standard for Paul, as Lawrence's own explicit theme-statement indicates – this time it is carried out in the novel. True, her determination that her sons *must* succeed for her has its ravaging effects. At the same time she alone is able to bring all their talents early into play, to understand them, stimulate and develop them.

What Gertrude Morel is, then, contends in objectively presented fashion with what the world around her – the world of her sons, including their women – offers. That is why William's 'Gipsy' is seen to be a fribble and that is why her middle-class pretentiousness is shattered in the Morel household. That is why Paul approves his mother's strength, with all its attendant dangers, against the overgentleness of Mrs Leivers, which stimulates an opposing brutality in the Leivers men. That is why, too, the chivalric-Christian spirituality of Miriam, with its overtones of Spenser and Walter Scott, appears only a weakness against the robust Mrs Morel.

If the Morel sons realize that their own mother is a considerably more remarkable woman than any they meet outside the home, that awareness operates as a standard. They are all free – granted the deeply rooted restrictions any person carries from childhood to maturity – to discriminate, to judge, to decide. William has self-dependence at an early age, and when he moves to London he is entirely on his own. His woman fails for the family, not for Mrs Morel alone. Paul is more implicated with his mother after William's move to London, his unfortunate engagement to 'Gipsy', and his death. Paul finds it more difficult than William to keep his independence clean. But in the wave-like returns to his relationship with his mother, he holds in his mind an awareness of all possible contingencies in his affairs both with Miriam and with Clara. He is even aware, in the tangle of the Miriam affair, just how much his mother is implicated.

If the Gertrude Morel portion is the novel's undoubted success, the part given over to Miriam is the novel's failure. Here, for the first time, what is felt to be the distinctive pulse-beat in Lawrence's approach to fiction becomes only clogging repetition, unresolved and nagging. There are perhaps more episodes devoted to Miriam than to Mrs Morel; but the complex ambiguity, pressing toward resolution (but never achieving it), has in retrospect, and even in close examination, the effect of a blur.

The beginning of that tortured and unsatisfactory account promises. After all, the lovers are of an age, both from homes embodying the best in working-class traditions – the farm and the mine. They enjoy relatively the same background in education

(Paul has the advantage here), reading, and 'chapel' associations. Paul 'was conscious only when stimulated. A sketch finished, he always wanted to take it to Miriam. In contact with Miriam he gained insight; his vision went deeper. 'From his mother he drew the life-warmth, the strength to produce; Miriam urged this warmth into intensity like a white light.' Miriam is his first love and so shares with him the impressionable years of growing up. They have even the same leisure amusements. True, the burden of the 'giving' comes from Paul: Miriam lives through him. He shows an aliveness to ideas and to the natural world, a quick perception of other peoples' natures, and a sensitivity that she can only appreciate, not return in kind. But even this, in its subtle way, ought to have prospered in a community where male ascendancy receives social support and is not seriously questioned, even by Clara.

But a relation as fevered as this comes to be must go one way or the other. It is the novel's great weakness that, in accounting for the defeat of Miriam, the reader is driven, ultimately, to the kind of ambiguity that is clarified only by biography, if even there. The reader is forced to say, for example, that Paul probably felt it in his marrow that this was not his woman – and let it go at that.

Conscious reason, of course, supports what strikes the reader as unconscious rejection. Paul cannot tolerate the romantic religious mystic in Miriam, who is victimized by her mother into the conviction that ' "There is one thing in marriage that is always dreadful, but you have to bear it." And I believed it.' In Miriam's presence, 'It could never be mentioned that the mare was in foal.' Even at the most relaxed moment of her final sexual surrender to Paul, the act has about it the explicit quality of 'surrender'. Miriam's 'spirituality' extends, however, to the world outside sex. Her religiose intensities characterize the simplest acts. Perhaps most maddeningly of all for Paul, her encouragement of his painting and of his ideas has about it the sucking, parasitic quality that Mrs Morel senses and hates. It operates in effect as the subtlest kind of flattery, one which drains his manliness and brings Paul under Miriam's control. As the inevitable result of his mother's example, Paul wants a woman who opposes him, fights him, questions him, challenges his maleness into vigorous proof. And this Miriam could not do.

But an indefinable sense of guilt spills over from the novel into biography. Paul 'uses' Miriam, almost, in his growing self-awareness and consciousness of gift. He places the girl in an awkward situation in her home and in the community, even though he realizes his cruelty and tries to make amends. Their friendship continues for years, so that he feels in the end that he *ought* to marry her for decency's sake, in the same way he feels that they ought to become engaged once their relationship is felt to be a serious one by both families. At the same time, Miriam has her own kind of independence and strength of character that refuses such terms. The situation is not simple. Above all, there is the complicating, *perhaps* decisive, factor of his mother's relentless opposition, but the novel itself fails disastrously to develop this sub-theme in a way to compel the irresistible judgment.

In the end we are forced to say that no single scene, and no cumulation of scenes, accounts for the final break. The defeat of Miriam fritters to a most unconvincing series of 'perhapses', fatally for the 'Miriam' portion of the novel: 'Perhaps he could not love her. Perhaps she had not in herself that which he wanted. It was the deepest motive of her soul, this self-mistrust. It was so deep she dared neither realize nor acknowledge it. Perhaps she was sufficient.'

### III

The Lawrence of affinities with the Blake who explored his age deeply and prophetically – as his novels *The Rainbow* and *Women in Love* clearly show – appears only under the surface of *Sons and Lovers*. Even in *Sons and Lovers*, however, the later and greater Lawrence is evident. He is there in the distinctive vitality, the compelling theme that thrusts forward into expression; he is there in the total absence of contrivance. He is there, too, in the rhythmic control of theme, intelligence controlling the blood-beat. There are as well magnificent scenes, with symbolism used as integrally and as skillfully as in the later novels. The reader may recall two instances among many: the one in which Paul makes a trip to Clifton Grove with Clara, when the river Trent figures turbulently in their passion; another when Paul is walking with Clara and Miriam, and Lawrence uses the stallion to symbolize his relationship with Clara, and uses flowers to objectify the considerably milder sexual attraction of Miriam.

In *Sons and Lovers*, however, Lawrence chooses to restrict his theme. It touches only *certain* major twentieth-century preoccupations, especially the Freudian. Had Lawrence developed the subordinate theme of *Sons and Lovers*, as he does in his later work, that novel might have explored the plight of his English civilization. *Sons and Lovers* might then have been a novel of major proportions. Indeed, we might see foreshadowings.

In *Sons and Lovers* Paul is the artist who earns his self-identity by defining himself against his complex society: home, the mining community, industrial England, religious belief and action, the educational system, the 'natural' world, and the farming community. That theme, however, is kept rigorously subordinate to the Freudian. In *Women in Love*, the case is different. Lawrence's eye is still impersonally on the object, and his tracing of that object – usually the relationship of a man and a woman – is as careful and as responsible as in *Sons and Lovers*. Whenever the development of his theme dictates, he will 'do' a scene in the manner of *Sons and Lovers*, only more skilfully, with surer and finer discriminations. The language he uses is still – and remains throughout a lifetime – vigorous, idiomatic, capable of any subtlety he wishes to communicate. He shows the same ability to follow a relationship, with intensities, recoils, doubts, violences, gradual involvement, intervals of tense serenity, all dramatically enacted within the flexible framework of a distinctive rhythmic structure. A combination of intense aliveness and minute notation characterizes his awareness of the natural world. We respect Lawrence because he remains, in his best work, the great novelist.

But after *Sons and Lovers* his major preoccupation, growing almost empirically from what he has so carefully perceived in his personal and communal world, begins to take discernible shape. Now he appears to explore principally the potential for living, the quality and degree of aliveness of representative English people to central, passional experience: the sex experience, human relations, the sensuous world, the vital, nonspecialized aspects of one's dedicated work. He sees himself and his people as heirs of a rich tradition – religious, vocational or craft, educational, and literary. In what ways, his novels and short stories appear implicitly to ask, is that tradition alive? In what ways does it transform what each individual represents at the center, or to what extent does it assert itself imperiously as a living standard? What margin for vitality, for creativity, does it allow? In what ways has it decayed irrevocably? *Sons and Lovers* only implies the disaster: in the dissatisfactions both Paul and (to a lesser degree) Miriam feel with community life, in Paul's questioning of inherited religious belief, in the way in which Walter Morel and Baxter Dawes are devirilized in their occupations.

Or to put it another way: Lawrence concentrates relentlessly on what makes men men, what makes women women in our industrialized, urbanized, scientifically controlled, moneyed society. He will try to understand the ways in which they are alive or dead – alive in their self-pride, their self-dignity, their capacity for 'living on the spot', Lawrence's own great gift. Through these individuals he will examine the traditions and institutions that they embody and that support them. In so far as these institutions support a vital principle that shows in speech, action, discrimination, in the quality of sexual, family, and communal relationships, shows even in clothes and furniture, they will win his novelist's allegiance. In so far as these institutions support the mechanical, the vestigial or merely habitual, the trivial, the intellectually specialized without wholeness, the vicious, or the degrading, they will stimulate all the intricate degrees and complexities of anger and contempt his art is capable of communicating.

Lawrence's work becomes indirectly an indictment of twentieth-century English civilization, but proceeds, in the better novels and short stories, entirely by characters realized in fictional relationships. In *Women in Love*, for example, he explores the industrial Midlands in historic scope, its society from top to bottom, its education, its 'scientific' world as it chokes the natural world; and he explores the Bohemian community of London. He examines all with a richness of organization that F. R. Leavis demonstrates in detail in his recent three-part analysis in *Scrutiny* (XVII 3 and 4; XVIII 1). And in *Women in Love* the individual's potency in the sexual relation reflects directly his potency as a *communal* being, with a function and a place in his community and in his larger society. The mature sex relation is grounded not only in the centrality of the physical passion. It is even more deeply rooted in mutual self-respect, self-dependence, and self-pride. The respect the principal characters enjoy derives almost wholly from the rôle they are allowed to play, the importance that society attaches to the rôle, but, most of all, in the intrinsic vitality and dignity of that rôle as the finest intelligence, the great artist's, measures it.

Lawrence, then, cuts behind the sexual relations to the positive margin for constructive action that his industrialized England permitted. By tracing with subtlety and care, in a firm and ordered exploration, the way of life of men on whom the continuity of the best traditions depended, he indicated implicitly the disintegration of that collective tradition. He fixed his novelist's eye on the destruction of England by the industrial revolution: the tragic ineffectualness of religion to control its abuses; the physical and moral ugliness it produced as it reduced the lives of most people to mechanisms in mechanized surroundings, and in placing in control of these machines people who were in turn controlled by the vast machinery; the pervasive substitution of degrading commercial valuations for valuations of community decency and responsibility, as well as for the richer community life of England of the past.

*Sons and Lovers* is a purgation become the successful work of art. The best of Lawrence's later works are, in similar fashion, acts of purgation. But this time the 'sickness of a whole civilization' is the true theme. We see it clearly revealed in his contention that 'the sexes are not by nature pitted against one another in hostility. It only happens so, in certain periods: when man loses his unconscious faith in himself, and woman loses faith in him, unconsciously, then consciously. It is not biological sex struggle. Not at all. Sex is the great uniter, the great unifier. Only in periods of the collapse of instinctive life-assurance in men does sex become a great weapon and divider.' He saw in later years that what ailed him was 'the absolute frustration of my primeval societal instinct. The hero illusion starts with the individualist illusion, and all resistances ensue. I think societal instinct much deeper than sex instinct – and society repression much more devastating.' It is Lawrence's distinction to have created great novels out of this tension.

# Frank O'Connor

## SONS AND LOVERS (1955)

WHEN we look at the last complete period of the novel, we find such names as Marcel Proust, James Joyce, André Gide, D. H. Lawrence, E. M. Forster, Thomas Mann, and Virginia Woolf.

And we are at once pulled up because at least four of the principal figures did not write novels at all. They wrote autobiography more or less thinly disguised as fiction. Another characteristic of this quartet is that none of them seems to have been sexually normal. All fell deeply under the influence of their mothers; Gide and Proust remained homosexual for their entire lives; Lawrence showed strongly marked homosexual tendencies, while Joyce's work covers practically every known form of sexual deviation. The only subject that none of them could apparently treat was normal heterosexual love.

Now, this can scarcely be a coincidence, and when we examine their work and find that even the types of deviation resemble one another, we are forced to the conclusion that there must be a common element that makes their authors react in this particular way.

Let us look first at Lawrence's *Sons and Lovers,* which is particularly interesting because, though it ends as a novel of the modern type, it begins as one of the classical kind, made familiar to us by nineteenth-century novelists.

To begin with, we have to notice that it is the work of one of the New Men who are largely a creation of the Education Act of 1870. Besides, we must note that it comes from the English Midlands, the industrial area. Naturally, the two facts are linked, and they represent a cultural shift not only from the middle to the working classes, but also from the area of wealth to the area of industry. The young people in the book are full of literary allusions that are not merely the self-conscious showing off of a young literary man, but represent the whole struggle of the working classes for culture. There is the same atmosphere in C. P. Snow's *Strangers and Brothers*, and for a similar reason.

It indicates too the dangers of such a shift of attitudes, for the Midlands, at least to a foreigner like myself, seem to be a different country altogether from the South of England, and even at times to resemble Ireland more than England. They are dissenting in religion, socialist in politics, and with a way of life which – again to a foreigner – seems full of dignity and even beauty. And, again, it is worth remembering that one of Lawrence's best stories, 'Odour of Chrysanthemums', which describes a miner's death, is not only quite unlike any other English story: though the critics have failed to notice it, it is also a very careful pastiche of Synge's *Riders to the Sea*. It suggests that young people of Lawrence's period did apparently recognize that in some ways their life was closer to Irish than to English ways, and that if it was to be given its full dignity, it had to be approached from an Irish standpoint.

But – and this is Lawrence's tragedy – it reminds us too that, unlike Ireland, the Midlands have no cultural capital, and that a young man of genius is necessarily driven to London, where he may learn only too quickly to despise the standards of his own people. This is not true of everybody, but of Lawrence it certainly is true. London acquaintances thought him something of a bounder and a cad. The family described under the name of Leivers in *Sons and Lovers* certainly did not think him either. It is the tragedy of William in the same novel. In later years Lawrence is the homeless, rootless man of letters drifting from country to country, continent to continent, writing with unfailing energy and brilliance, but never with the intensity displayed in *Sons and Lovers* and some of his early stories.

The break with his roots occurred during the writing of the novel, and it is plain for anyone who will take the trouble to read it carefully. Absolutely, the opening half is the greatest thing in English fiction. It has all the brilliance of *Pride and Prejudice* and the opening of *Middlemarch* with the tragic power of certain

scenes in *The Last Chronicle*. Put in its simplest form, it is the
dilemma of a sensitive boy between the conflicting claims of
mother and sweetheart. This adds a new element of tragedy to
the novel, for, despite the universal quality of the theme, it is an
element that could only have come from the New Men and the
industrial areas, for it is only in those surroundings that a boy is
forced to recognize the spiritual achievement of motherhood. A
hundred pounds a year would have been sufficient to mask the
whole achievement and tragedy of Mrs Morel. Even a difference
in class would have done so, for, greatly as Mrs Crawley is
drawn by Trollope, her struggle is presented as it appeared to a
member of the upper classes: a sordid, unnecessary, *imposed*
ordeal. In Lawrence, poverty is treated as a necessary condition of
life, and it is by means of the explicit exiguous budgets that we
are made to appreciate the full significance of Mrs Morel's
attempts to create order and beauty about her, and the delight
and anguish these could bring to a sensitive boy. We *respect* Mrs
Crawley's struggle to find necessities for her family; we *rejoice*
in the glorious scene in which Mrs Morel gives rein to her wicked
extravagance and comes home clutching a pot that cost her
fivepence and a bunch of pansies and daisies that cost her four-
pence.

Again it is the Midland background that gives significance to
Miriam's passion for culture, this, too, a struggle toward the light,
though of a different kind. As we are made to feel the weight of
Morel's physical violence and the brutality of the mines crushing
down like a leaden sky, so too we feel with almost agonizing
intensity the upward movement in chapel, school, and home, the
passion of desire to 'build Jerusalem in England's green and
pleasant land'. Nature is not, as in Hardy, a dark background to a
gloomy fate, but an upward surging like music, poetry, religion.
No other novel is so filled with flowers. When in a novel for the
leisured classes someone talks of Rilke, or a Picasso print, or
carnations, one's tendency is to groan: 'Holy Smoke, he's off
again!' But we rejoice in Mrs Morel's little triumph over the pot-
man, in Miriam's algebra lesson, in Mrs Morel's three little bulbs
under the hedge. These are no longer the negatives of dandyism

or the neutrals of an educated class, but the positive achievements of a life with a sense of purpose and direction, lived by people who are complete moral entities. Joyce, too, had known the same thing, and in the terrible little scene in *Ulysses* when Dedalus's ragged sister covets the secondhand French grammar, he makes us feel it, but we feel it rather as an icy clutch on our hearts than as a moment of rejoicing in man's passionate desire to transcend himself. Joyce's Dublin was a place without signposts. Again, his poverty is pathetic rather than tragic.

It is hard to criticize this matchless book, yet there *is* something wrong with it, and, whatever it may be, it is the same thing that is wrong with Lawrence himself and that turns him into a homeless man of letters, and it is here, under our eyes, that the smash occurs if only we could see what it is. What I mean is not a literary fault, or is so only in a secondary sense. It would be only natural that a young man's book should contain shifting planes, particularly when all the significant scenes are written with such explosive power that it is a miracle when he recovers any sense of direction at all. No, the smash is a psychological one and inherent in the situation that he describes rather than in the technique he uses to describe it. It is inherent in the situation of the young man torn between his mother and Miriam, both of whom want the same thing from him.

There is almost certainly a false note in the chapters describing Miriam as Paul Morel's mistress. I do not know if in real life Lawrence was actually the lover of the girl he describes as Miriam, nor am I greatly concerned about the question. But the situation of the novel implies that they could never have been lovers, and that this was in fact the thing that drove Paul to Clara. The trouble with the Oedipal relationship is that it specializes the sexual instinct. Sexual contact is the only thing lacking between the boy and his mother, and he tends to seek this in a form where it implies nothing else, where it does not produce an actual feeling of betrayal of the mother – in Gogol in the form of self-abuse, in Proust in the form of homosexuality. Human love – the type represented by Miriam – is bound to represent a betrayal of the mother, because the love is identical except for this one slight specialized thing. Miriam is his mother's rival because the love that she offers is human love; Clara is not because the love that she offers is in fact a non-human love.

Clara is non-human in the same way as every single woman whom Lawrence described after the writing of this book is non-human. None of them is allowed to challenge the image of his mother in humanity. And this is where we come to the really pathological streak in the book. Clara is a married woman whose husband is a smith in the surgical-appliance store where Paul is employed, and immediately she appears in the novel her husband appears also. He hates Paul long before Paul becomes the lover of his wife. When Paul and she become friendly, Paul presses her with questions about her relations with Dawes. He even has a fight with Dawes, and later goes to visit him in the hospital and makes friends with him. The two men have a peculiar relationship centered on their common possession of Clara, and finally Paul brings about the reunion of husband and wife.

Now, these chapters, which occupy a considerable part of the last half of the book, have nothing whatever to do with the subject of the novel – at least on the surface. They might easily belong to an entirely different novel. Indeed, they might be about different characters, for from this point onward Paul is referred to as 'Morel', a name which has so far been associated only with his father, so that we even get superficially confused in our reading. Lawrence's original intention is fairly clear. It was to present Miriam not as a type of human love, but as a type of spiritual love, Clara as a type of sensual love, neither of which can satisfy the heart of the young man who loves his mother. This design has been obscured by the irrelevant physical relations with Miriam on the one hand, and on the other by the emphasis laid on Clara's husband as opposed to Clara herself. But that is only part of the trouble. The real trouble is that Paul Morel is not in love with Clara, but with Dawes. Subject and object have again changed places, and we are back with the old extraordinary theme of *The Eternal Husband*. That this is not merely a personal and perverse reading of the strained melodrama imposed on a young man of genius by his lack of experience will be clear to anyone who knows his Lawrence, for the theme occurs again and again in his later work. The most interesting example is an early story, 'The Shades of Spring', in which the girl we have come to know as Miriam is shown after her young man's desertion of her. She has now become engaged to a second man, and the story describes the odd attraction that the first feels for him. It is most explicit in 'Jimmy and the Desperate Woman', where Lawrence recognizes in the person of another man of slightly effeminate tastes the attraction of a physically powerful husband transmitted through the wife. The biographers tell us that the hero of the story is Middleton Murry, which merely indicates how incapable Lawrence became of drawing any character objectively: he can only attribute to him his own peculiar weakness. The whole passage is worth considering again in context.

And, as he sat in the taxi, a perverse but intense desire for her came over him, making him almost helpless. He could feel, so strongly, the presence of that other man about her, and this went to his head like neat spirits. That other man! In some subtle, inexplicable way he was actually bodily present, the husband. The woman moved in his aura. She was hopelessly married to him.

And this went to Jimmy's head like neat whiskey. Which of the two would fall before him with a greater fall – the woman, or the man, her husband?

It is hard to know what the real origin of this perverse attraction in Lawrence represents. That it existed in him in real life we may safely deduce from Murry's remark – made in all innocence of the meaning of the texts I have quoted – that Lawrence was attracted to Frieda's husband almost as much as to Frieda. Obviously the attraction is homosexual, but that word is so loosely and coarsely abused that it can scarcely be applied without misgivings to a noble and refined personality like Lawrence's. It is certainly linked with his adoration of his mother, and it seems as though the link must be a specialized form of sexuality which excludes the spiritual element merely because it would then become a rival to mother love. At the same time the figure of the father, consciously excluded by the boy, would seem to return in an unrecognizable, unconscious form and take its place in the relationship with the woman. If one accepts this reading of it (and it is as tentative as any reading of an analogical situation must be), Dawes is really Paul's father, and Paul, through his relationship with Clara, which gives him the opportunity of probing Dawes's relations with his wife, is not only able to repeat the offense against his father by robbing him of his wife, but is also, in the manner of a fairy tale, able to undo the wrong by reconciling them. It is a beautiful example of the dual function of such analogical relationships.

Whatever the origin of the situation, it is the key to Lawrence's work. His rejection of Miriam is a rejection of masculinity in himself, and after it he is condemned to write only of those things which the feminine side of his character permits him to write of. He is an intuitive writer by sheer necessity. To Edward Garnett he defended his new, non-human form of writing by the pretense that the old sort of realistic writing which Garnett understood was out of date, but that his own choice of his sort of writing took place only after *Sons and Lovers* is clearly untrue. The choice was made during the actual writing, and the result is the Clara Dawes section, the end of the old Lawrence and the beginning of the new.

Not that he may not have felt the necessity, for all over Europe the old human conception of character was breaking down. Character in Turgenev and Trollope exists as an extension, by virtue of its predictability. All their great characters have been lived with. They are regarded, rightly or wrongly, as being essentially knowable. When Joyce uses the word 'epiphany', 'a showing forth', for the themes of his own stories, he indicates already that the temporal, objective conception of character no longer exists, and that it can be apprehended only in moments when it unconsciously betrays itself. Virginia Woolf, too, insists on this moment of revelation, and, like Joyce, she writes the typical one-day novel of the period. The day itself is regarded as an epiphany. Proust's characters are all perceived in such moments, and nothing that we have learned about them at one moment gives us the least indication of what they may be like in another. It is, of course, a view, deeply influenced by Freud's theories, which make the character unknowable except to the analyst; it is even, in many of the writers of the time, a view motivated by the furtiveness and secrecy of the homosexual, yet in the light of history it is so much a response to all that has gone before that one cannot help wondering whether even Freud and the homosexuals are not themselves mere symptoms of something taking place entirely in the mind.

# Graham Hough

# ADOLESCENT LOVE (1956)

THE Paul and Miriam chapters are the essential core of *Sons and Lovers*. Adolescent love has been treated in fiction both before and since, tenderly or ironically; but never with such penetration, so little sentimentality or such honest determination to show its nature and the corruptions to which it is subject. Lawrence takes it seriously, and this is rarely done; and he treats it, under the pressure of an urgent personal necessity, from the inside. But quantitatively the Miriam relationship occupies only about a third of the book. The letter to Garnett, after describing the battle between the mother and Miriam for the soul of Paul, continues: 'The son decides to leave his soul in his mother's hands, and like his elder brother, go for passion.' But this, with other passages in the commentary, is not quite borne out by the text. It is wisdom after the event. At the end of the 'Defeat of Miriam' chapter Paul recognises that he cannot love her physically, but he does not know why. He does not clearly recognise the power of the mother-image. It is true that he returns to his mother; the seal is set on his return by their trip to Lincoln together, in which he treats her like 'a fellow taking his girl for an outing'. But he thinks that he is still faithful to Miriam, that she still holds him in the depths of his soul. Yet her possession of his soul comes to matter less and less, for at the same time another woman is arousing his physical passion.

Clara Dawes represents all that Miriam does not. She is independent, emancipated, experienced and physically uninhibited. She is also separated from her husband, whom she has written off as an insensitive brute. While Miriam trespasses on the sanctities that had been the mother's preserve, Clara Dawes stands freely on unoccupied ground. Miriam wants a completely committed love – with all its concomitants of fidelity, tenderness and understanding. This Paul cannot give; his fidelity and tenderness are already bespoken; and Miriam is condemned to sterile conflict. But Clara's is a frank, physical appeal. The temperamental difference is subtly emphasised. Shortly before his first meeting with Clara, Paul has been reading the Bible to Miriam, and he boggles at a passage about a woman in travail. Anything suggesting the physical relation of man and woman is taboo between them. Not long after, when they are walking with Clara, they meet an elderly spinster lovingly caressing a great horse. They find her odd, and Clara blurts out flatly, 'I suppose she wants a man'. Immediately after as he sees Clara striding ahead, Paul feels a hot wave of excitement run through him.

The excitement grows. Paul drifts away from Miriam into a Socialist-Suffragette-Unitarian group around Clara. She comes to work under Paul in the factory where he is employed, and her husband also works there. The development of their relation is wholly without the tender pastoral glow of the farmhouse idyll with Miriam, but also, in spite of obvious complications, without the hidden obstacles and inhibitions. He does not even realise at first that he desires her sexually.

Sex had become so complicated in him that he would have denied that he ever could want Clara or Miriam or any woman whom he *knew*. Sex desire was a sort of detached thing, that did not belong to a woman. He loved Miriam with his soul. He grew warm at the thought of Clara, he battled with her, he knew the curves of her breast and shoulders as if they had been moulded inside him; and yet he did not positively desire her. He would have denied it for ever. (ch. x)

His mother is not displeased; she thinks he is getting away from Miriam. And even Miriam is little disturbed by the new situation; she is sure there is nothing in it.

Miriam knew how strong was the attraction of Clara for him; but still she was certain that the best in him would triumph. His feeling for Mrs Dawes – who, moreover, was a married woman – was shallow and temporal, compared with his love for herself. He would come back to her, she was sure. (ch. x)

Yet she is afraid to let Paul become her lover, and he can never bring himself to push things to a crisis. The situation between them grows steadily more unsatisfactory. Paul's physical desires are becoming more importunate, and it seems on the face of things that it is Miriam's reluctance which stands in the way. We may read between the lines that her reluctance is the consequence of his earlier inhibitions; but this is never said. And from this time on the suspicion obtrudes itself that the author is identifying himself too closely with Paul's point of view. The truth of the presentation is not impaired, as far as it goes; but less than justice is done to Miriam's side, and Paul's *ex parte* explanations have it too much their own way, as they did not in the earlier chapters of the story. Eventually he breaks with her, after eight years of friendship and love.

Of course he goes straight to Clara; and easily, naturally, without forethought or complication, he has of her what he has wanted for years. Their first encounter is not even described. Paul has not yet realised that women need to be satisfied as well as men relieved, and at the time of writing Lawrence probably shared his ignorance. At any rate, he is not at the stage when he wishes to analyse and differentiate sexual experience. The mere fact of its occurrence is enough. Paul is immensely elated. He takes Clara to tea with his mother, without embarrassment, and his mother thinks, 'What a man he seems.' He is growing up, and the mists that clung round the Miriam relationship have cleared. Even on Clara's visits to the Morel household 'it was a clear, cool atmosphere, where everyone was himself and in harmony'. Paul still sees Miriam, but now his bitter comment on the affair is that it was only talk – 'There never *was* a great deal more than talk between us.' The sense of tension relieved is vivid enough; but we are obstinately left with the impression that Lawrence does not want to convey – that the relation with Miriam was far the stronger and more meaningful of the two. There is a slightly smug satisfaction about Paul, for having got what he wants without forfeiting his mother's approval, in which the author seems at least partly implicated. It is not the women whom their sons sleep with that possessive mothers hate – it is the women whom they love; and it is not hard to see here the cause for Jessie Chambers' charge of capitulation to the mother's point of view.

Paul has at last succeeded in finding pleasure without the sense of guilt; and his need for this is probably the key to another curious episode, otherwise hard to explain. Baxter Dawes, Clara's husband, has degenerated into a drunken bully. He wants his revenge on Paul, waylays him and beats him up. Paul is severely hurt and becomes ill as a result. Pneumonia follows, and while his mother nurses him, both Clara and Miriam are rejected. Paul has had his pleasure, allowed himself to be punished for it, and now returns safely to his mother's care. But it is too late. Immediately afterwards his mother's illness declares itself; it is a fatal cancer. Paul is prostrated with grief. While visiting his mother in hospital, he learns that Dawes is there, too, and he goes to visit him. Between typhoid and drink, Dawes is brought pretty low, and the two meet on the ground of their common misery. A sort of friendship develops between them, and a little later we have the curious situation of Paul's suggesting to Clara that she has used her husband badly. Clara is even inclined to agree with him. Paul is so broken by his mother's illness that he becomes indifferent to Clara, and she begins to tire of him. He tells Dawes that she has finished with him. During the last days of his mother's illness he sees little of Clara and Miriam, and they mean nothing to him when he does; but his rôle as Dawes' friend and protector continues to develop. He visits him in a convalescent home, tries to cheer him up and give him the courage to start in life again. Paul says that he feels in a worse mess than Dawes – 'in a tangled sort of hole, rather dark and dreary, and no road anywhere'. Paul indeed is withering away. Clara joins them, and she finds Paul paltry and insignificant, finds that her husband in his defeat has more manly dignity – even a certain nobility. Paul is convinced that he is finished, and in a final act of self-negation he slips away and leaves the two together. And it does not take Clara long to recognise her real mate.

'Take me back!' she whispered, ecstatic. 'Take me back, take me back!' And she put her fingers through his fine, thin dark hair, as if she were only semi-conscious. He tightened his grasp on her. (ch. xiv)

So Paul is cleared of his only real sexual relation, and the bond with the dead mother is unimpaired.

A last effort with Miriam fails. They meet again, with all the old tension. She suggests marriage, and in a scene of tortured, enigmatic confusion he rejects it. The situation hardly explains itself – or rather, two inconsistent explanations are offered. Paul says: 'You love me so much, you want to put me in your pocket. And I should die there, smothered.' But we are also told that he longs for the comfort and understanding she could give him, and wants her to take possession of him, as it were by force; she will not take that initiative, and as long as the decision rests with him he cannot make it. Again we are placed at the centre of the entanglement, with all the blindness and lack of comprehension that this implies. It is hard to resist the conviction that there is some impurity of motive here. It is as though Lawrence himself is forcing the blame on Miriam for refusing to live Paul's life for him. Paul has been growing weaker and less positive since his first rejection of Miriam. This is the climax of his nullity, and invites the final condemnation of his neurotic refusal of responsibility for his own existence.

Lawrence studiously avoids all attempts at such a final judgment. We are familiar, in the more developed kinds of novel, with the spectator character who stands apart from the action and serves as a vehicle for the novelist's point of view. There is no such character in *Sons and Lovers*. No one is right. No one can claim a superior insight to the others. All the main characters – Paul, Miriam, Mrs Morel, Clara Dawes – make extremely penetrating remarks on each other. All are blind to much that is going on around them. Even Lawrence the author, whom we must distinguish from his own portrait of himself in Paul, is not in this position. Lawrence's exposition of the novel closes with these words: 'He is left in the end naked of everything, with the drift towards death.' But never trust the author, trust the tale, as Lawrence himself said. What does the tale actually tell us? It has not often been observed (Anthony West, I believe, is alone in calling attention to it)\* that at the ghastly climax of his mother's illness Paul, with the connivance of his sister, kills her with an overdose of sleeping tablets to spare her further agony. Realistically considered, it is simply an act of despairing mercy. Symbolically, it has another significance. Here, where the regression of Paul's character has reached its farthest point, there is still something within him which is capable of decisive action – capable even of killing the mother to whom he is bound, to liberate both of them and to end her agony and his. And this prepares us for the actual end of the novel, which is not as Lawrence describes it, but as follows:

'Mother!' he whispered – 'mother!'
She was the only thing that held him up, himself, amid all this. And she was gone, intermingled herself. He wanted her to touch him, have him alongside with her.
But no, he would not give in. Turning sharply, he walked towards the city's gold phosphorescence. His fists were shut, his mouth set fast. He would not take that direction, to the darkness, to follow her. He walked towards the faintly humming, glowing town, quickly.

In fact, he refuses to give in and the final motion is towards life. Paul, whose vacillations and refusals have worn him away till he has reached something like nonentity, proves in the end capable of a regenerating spark. At whatever cost to himself and others he has kept his frail independence alive. And then he puts the whole imbroglio behind him as Lawrence was putting it behind him by writing the book.

'The novels and stories come unwatched out of one's pen.' And Lawrence the man is not clearly aware of what has come from the pen of Lawrence the writer. Lawrence the writer, at any rate at this stage, fulfils the conditions demanded by Keats: he is 'capable of being in uncertainties, mysteries, doubts, without any irritable reaching after fact and reason'. The part of the book which is most contrived, most written to a thesis, is the love-affair with Clara Dawes. It represents, or is supposed to represent,

\* The reader will see from other essays in this volume that Mr Hough is mistaken in this belief. G.S.

Paul's attempt at a simple physical relationship as a relief from the obscure psychic complexities of the love between himself and Miriam. Yet it is far less powerful, far less successful, in expressing the essential nature of love than the unfulfilled and tormented passages with Miriam. Lawrence, in fact, is at his strongest when he is exploring a state of affairs which is obscure, which he has not exhausted in life. The writing is a catharsis. When a situation has been lived through and completed, his best and most characteristic powers are not called out. Lawrence's limited experience of mere physiological satisfaction without any stronger bond seems to have been completed before 1912; it never seems to have interested him much in life, and it provides no lasting satisfaction and no solution to the conflict in the novel. Indeed, the emptiness of the affair with Clara Dawes makes it an inadequate counterpoise to the relation with Miriam.

Again, like *The White Peacock*, a novel about frustration and failure and contradictions that are never reconciled. But in *The White Peacock* the human failures are almost absorbed in the quivering joy of earth, the vibration of the neo-human world that surrounds them. In *Sons and Lovers* the human conflicts have become more intense and more pressing, and the necessity for following them to a conclusion more absolute. The idyllic passages are not a diversion from the plot; they occur only in the Miriam episodes, and they are strictly subordinated to Miriam herself. They are the necessary setting for her character, and the shared love of Paul and Miriam for flowers, birds'-eggs and trees is only a pathetic extension of their feeling for each other. The intense realisation of personal forces burns away all the minor social falsities that impairs the reality of *The White Peacock*; and it also burns away most of the lyrical tenderness that makes that novel a springtime story in spite of the frustrations of the plot. So that *Sons and Lovers* becomes incidentally a full, intimate, sympathetic, but also a harsh and unrelieved presentation of working-class life – the oppressively close-knit family system, the narrow play for the individual sensibilities; the strength of individual development when it manages to survive among the massive forces that press upon it. Lawrence never captures this continuous sense of actuality in a novel again, though he does in some of the shorter tales. For this reason *Sons and Lovers* remains his masterpiece to those who abide by the central tradition of the novel. Possibly they are right, but those who hold this view are still not penetrating to what is essential in Lawrence. The naturalistic success of *Sons and Lovers* is only incidental; the growing point of the book is the psychological adventurousness, the resolute beginning of an exploration into the tangled relations between men and women. In his next two novels this is to be Lawrence's only theme.

*Simon Lesser*

# FORM AND ANXIETY (1957)

OF the already identified resources available to form for combating anxiety, we need remind ourselves of only one more: its capacity to keep the most frightening implications of its material from the attention of consciousness. Unpalatable matters may be disguised, but we shall not pause to consider the various means used to accomplish this. We are already familiar with some of them, and the subject of disguise is discussed elsewhere.[1] Furthermore, if by disguise we mean the deliberate, or even the pre-conscious or unconscious, *alteration* of material so that its real significance will not be perceived, though important it is far less important a device than was originally thought. Fiction seldom has to go this far out of its way to conceal anything. The language in which it is likely to be conceived and cast from the start – a language so natural to fiction that it has been accepted unthinkingly by generations of storytellers and readers alike – tends by its very nature to inhibit the apprehension of anxiety-producing layers of meaning in conceptual terms. Fiction speaks to us in a language which *effortlessly* conceals many things from conscious awareness at the same time that it communicates them to the unconscious with extraordinary vividness.

I am by no means sure that I have succeeded in conveying the nature of this language or the extent to which fiction utilizes it. The concept of non-discursive communication is new in esthetic theory, and may not seem applicable to the literary arts since their medium is words. But anyone can quickly acquire an appreciation of the difference between the language of fiction and ordinary conceptual discourse by undertaking a simple and pleasant experiment. The experiment I propose is to read in

quick succession Freud's 'The Most Prevalent Form of Degradation in Erotic Life'[2] and D. H. Lawrence's *Sons and Lovers*. By
coincidence they were written at about the same time and published within a year of one another – the paper in 1912, the novel
in 1913. They have an almost schematic correspondence: they
both explore the painful opposition which arises in some men
between tender and sensual love – an opposition which may be so
extreme that, 'Where such men love they have no desire and
where they desire they cannot love.'[3] Both works show that the
primary factor to which this opposition can be traced is the
young boy's overattachment to the mother.

Despite the close relationship between the novel and the paper,
which could be developed in greater detail, *one could read the
former after reading the latter without becoming aware of it.* It is
necessary to read the novel in a way quite different from that in
which one ordinarily reads fiction – to have advance knowledge
of the parallels and to be looking for them – to become aware of
them during the act of reading. Is this because Lawrence learned
of Freud's ideas, or by coincidence had precisely the same ideas,
and then sought to embody them in a work of fiction which would
at the same time conceal them from awareness? Almost certainly
this is not the explanation. Lawrence may have never been aware
of some of the ideas to be found in his novel;* and he was not
primarily concerned with the ideas of which he was aware *as
ideas*, as abstract generalities. He was concerned with telling a
story – a story which grew out of his own experience and needs.
He was concerned with Paul Morel (behind whom it is impossible
not to discern Lawrence) and his mother and Miriam and
Clara. His story represents an attempt to imagine how matters
would have worked out among these people – and to some
extent, of course, to re-experience actual occurrences. Whatever

* There is no evidence, for example, that he recognized the extent to
which Paul's tie to his mother determined his very selection of Miriam
and his failure to respond to either Miriam or Clara in a way which did
justice to all their qualities. Lawrence did, however, recognize that
Paul was fettered to his mother and that this made it difficult for him
to establish a good relationship with any other woman. See *The Letters
of D. H. Lawrence*, ed. Aldous Huxley (New York, 1932) p. 78.

explanations are offered for his characters' conduct are intuitive, casual and fragmentary; very few generalizations are drawn.

It happens that the behavior of Lawrence's characters illustrates some of the very mechanisms Freud explains systematically in 'The Most Prevalent Form of Degradation in Erotic Life'. From Lawrence's novel the dissecting intelligence of the critic can abstract the main ideas Freud develops in his paper; and it is worthwhile to abstract them – doing so may help the critic to crystallize certain of his impressions of the book. But whereas Freud labored to bring his ideas before us as clearly as possible, it would not be an exaggeration to say that Lawrence was determined that we should *not* have 'ideas', that we should not think conceptually, as we read his story. More accurately, he had a different objective: to engage us emotionally, to induce us to share the experiences of his characters; and he intuitively recognized that he could not achieve this objective if he spoke to the intellect alone. Lawrence himself, as Aldous Huxley has pointed out, 'refused to know abstractly'.[4] As man and as artist, he felt driven to render his story with as much concreteness, vividness and immediacy as he could muster. The scenes and incidents must speak for themselves, and they speak in a language which is vaguer but richer and more stirring than the language of intellectual discourse.

There is no word which will quite do justice to the way the language he employs is apprehended. Consider the scene where Paul, walking in his mother's garden at night, decides finally to give up Miriam. It is apparent enough that we do not formulate the meaning of this scene; how can one formulate the precise significance of the scent of a flower? Nor is it quite accurate to say that we *infer* what is going on in Paul; the word implies a more purposive kind of intellectual activity and a greater gulf between reader and character than actually obtains at this point. Even the word *sense* implies such a gulf. If we are absorbed in the novel, we are emphatically linked with Paul, we feel what he feels, we are affected as he is affected by the sights, smells and sounds which assail him. It would be redundant and, we sense, a profanation to state what we feel in words.

In a sense it is foolish to compare paper and novel, they are incommensurate; but the reading of both in quick succession is likely to give us increased respect for the capacity of fiction to deal with potentially disturbing material without arousing anxiety. Freud's essay may make us squirm at times. There is some evidence that one of the statements his argument demanded caused him to recoil, despite his scientific detachment and long habit of confronting the facts about man's nature, however repugnant they might be. Though the novel gives us an experience of greater immediacy and intensity than the paper, it produces less of that disquiet which is a sign of inner anxiety. Of course, the sensory language of fiction, of which Lawrence was such a master, is only one of the factors responsible for this achievement.

## NOTES

1. See, for example, Marie Bonaparte, *The Life and Works of Edgar Allan Poe* (1949), especially pp. 642–8.
2. *Collected Papers*, IV (1948).
3. Ibid., p. 207.
4. Ibid., p. xv.

# David Daiches

# LAWRENCE AND THE FORM OF THE NOVEL (1960)

*Ulysses* baffled many people and angered many more; but nobody mistook it for a novel like *The Mill on the Floss*. In this respect D. H. Lawrence was less lucky than Joyce; for his greatest, most original, and most characteristic work could be and often was mistaken for something like *The Mill on the Floss*, even by many of those who professed to admire him. In his mature novels Lawrence was at least as revolutionary as Joyce in the conception of prose fiction which he was acting out, but he was not involved in those problems of time and consciousness which Joyce and Virginia Woolf saw as paramount and which had such an immediately visible effect on those writers' technique. It is therefore less easy to fit Lawrence into any obvious scheme of 'the modern novel'. He remains, however, a great innovator, one who put the novel form to genuinely new uses and broke out of the limits imposed on story-telling by two hundred years of prose fiction to confound the categories of critics and discover new ways of presenting a strong individual vision of life through the deployment of incident in narrative.

Though Lawrence began with conventional ideas of what the novel was and ought to be, it was not long before he gave signs of seeing it as capable of doing many more things than those to which it had hitherto been confined. 'You can put anything you like in a novel. So why do people *always* go on putting the same thing? Why is the *vol au vent* always chicken!' So wrote Lawrence in 1925, defending in his characteristically breezy and colloquial way his own practice in using the novel for any purpose that appealed to him. For the novel attracted Lawrence as the appropriate literary form for him to use just because he saw it as so undefined, so free, so capable of testing out a vision of life without rigidly limiting oneself to it. 'The novel is the highest form of human expression so far attained. Why? Because it is so incapable of the absolute.' This remark, from the same essay, must be set beside Lawrence's prophetic utterances and his violent preaching to his generation if we are not to confuse his aims as an artist with his aims as a sage. 'In a novel, everything is relative to everything else, if that novel is art at all. There may be didactic bits, but they aren't the novel.' One might almost say that for Lawrence the novel represents a tentative acting-out in the imagination of a vision or a series of visions of the true values involved in human relationships. 'Tell Arnold Bennett', he once wrote to his literary agent, 'that all rules of construction hold good only for novels that are copies of other novels. A book which is not a copy of other books has its own construction, and what he calls faults, he being an old imitator, is what I call characteristics.'

Lawrence's characteristic response to the dilemma of modern civilization as he saw it is not to seek ways of bridging the gap between private vision and public belief or to feel the breakdown of public belief as in any way inhibiting, which is what we see in most of the great innovating novelists of his generation. Nor is he a social reformer, seeking a blueprint of a new society within which the values he believed in could flourish. He soon came to feel the deadness of modern industrial civilization, with the mechanizing of personality, the corruption of the will, and the dominance of sterile intellect over the authentic inward passions of men, which he saw as the inevitable accompaniment of modern life. But he has no patience with political or social panaceas. Sometimes he talked as a wild anarchist, asserting that everything must be pulled down or blown up so that a new start might be made. But the vision conveyed by his characteristic novels is not political in any way, even in a destructive anarchist way. He is concerned always with human relationships, with the relation of the self to other selves, with the possibilities of fulfilment of personality, and with exposing all the dead formulas – about romantic love, about friendship, about marriage, about the good life – which can cause so much deadness or frustration or distortion in the life of the individual. There is nearly always a strong autobiographical element in his novels; he never attempts, as Joyce does (and Joyce uses autobiography too but in a wholly different way), to construct a self-contained world outside himself and his readers with its own structure and its own *livableness*. He projects his novels from the very center of his own passionate experience so that they act out, sometimes tentatively, sometimes fiercely, sometimes desperately, his own deepest insights and forms of awareness, and the lyric and the dramatic modes interpenetrate each other.

If we say that Lawrence turned to the novel for its freedom and tentativeness, and if we contrast that freedom and that tentativeness with the violent self-assurance of his prophetic utterances, this does not mean that his activities as fictional artist and as prophet never get in each other's way. But this can be said: Lawrence is nearly always able to embody his vision of life in adequate artistic form when that vision is fully realized in his own mind and imagination; the murky symbolism, the hysterical tone, the bogus primitivism, and all the other elements in the novels that distress even admiring readers, arise from his own doubts of his own position. One can almost say that Lawrence protests too much when he has some deep inward uncertainty or confusion about what he really wants to say. And since, if he gave himself sufficient room to maneuver, he was always liable to move over into areas where he had this inward uncertainty or confusion, there is not a single one of his longer novels which is not flawed somewhere. His most perfect work is found among his short stories, where he can often embody a personally discovered truth about human relationships in a story superbly molded to embody precisely that truth with a combination of precision and power, of delicacy and urgency.

Lawrence was impelled always by his own relentless vision, which would not leave him alone and which would not let him leave other people alone. Son of a Midland miner and a genteel mother who fought all her married life to carry her children out of the working class, he saw life early in terms of a dialectic of coarseness and refinement which became progressively modified until it no longer implied the simple moral pattern he had first seen in it but a tortured paradigm of the psychological ills of modern civilization, which pushed vitality into insensitive brutality and intelligence into mechanical gentility. Even in *Sons and Lovers,* his first really successful novel (in the critical, not the commercial, sense), the division between the coarse, belligerently working-class father and the refined ambitious gentility of the mother is not a division between good and bad; though Lawrence thought at the time that he was lauding his mother and damning his father and though he later recanted and confessed that he had done his father a most grave injustice in not recognizing his genuine vitality and wholeness of personality, the fact is that any sensitive reader of the novel can see at once that the mother, for all the passionate and moving intimacy with which she is presented, stands in the long run for death, and the father, insofar as he is allowed to play any real part in the novel, stands in his own rather shabby way for life on such terms as life was available in a Midland mining village of that era. Against this pattern of vitality and gentility, with all the qualifications and modifications implied in the fact that the vitality was often mindless and brutal and the gentility often intelligent and sensitive, Lawrence sets the theme of the demanding mother who, having given up the prospect of achieving a true emotional life with her husband, turns to her sons and captures their manhood in her possessive love. With the death of the eldest son (a death for which, in some oblique but powerfully symbolic way, the loving mother is responsible), the younger son becomes the sole target of this compelling mother-love, and he responds with equal passion. The delicacy, tenderness, and sheer overwhelming sense of reality with which Lawrence presents the unfolding relationship of this mother and son make us lose any sense of moral judgment in pure implication in the action. The situation is, of course, autobiographical: in this aspect of the novel, at least, Lawrence was telling the story of his own relations with his mother and father. It is autobiographical in other elements too; the setting, presented with a most powerful sense of atmosphere and of physical detail, of the rhythm of work and

life in a miner's cottage, of the relation between the industrial
and the agricultural aspects of the landscape, helps to present the
very quality and reality of living in that place at that time and in
doing so makes implied comments on the state of early twentieth-
century England as well as on the relation between an industrial
future and an agricultural past. Much of Lawrence's fiercest and
deepest feelings in childhood went into *Sons and Lovers*: nostalgia is one of its many elements. Yet it is nevertheless fiction,
not autobiography, as we could have told even if the real character who appears in the novel as Miriam had not later written a
book to point out the differences between her relationship with
Lawrence in fact and Miriam's relationship with Paul Morel in the
novel. Paul is in love with Miriam, the daughter of a neighboring
farmer, and Miriam loves him; but the mother's love effectively
prevents Paul from achieving any adequate response to Miriam's
love or any adequate embodiment of his own love for Miriam:
Paul is led to seek satisfaction for his sexual appetite in more
casual ways, which his mother tolerates because they do not
threaten his status as *her* lover. The mother-son relationship
thus forces the son to (in Lawrence's own summary of the plot)
'go for passion' in his relations with other women, to attempt
nothing more than short-lived passionate sexual affairs. But this
is unsatisfactory to all concerned – to Paul, to Miriam, to the
girl on whom Paul vents his passion, to the mother – and in the
end the mother dies of cancer, almost, it seems, an act of despair
because she can no longer keep her son as her own unique, pure
lover. It is an act of near-despair on both sides, for Paul too is
unable to bear the situation and is so wrung by the protracted
agonies of his mother's dying that he hastens her death by giving
her an overdose of morphia in her milk.

Such a crude summary tells little about the quality of the book,
and least of all about the long central scenes between Paul and
Miriam where, we cannot help feeling, the fictional imagination is
working on autobiographical material in a peculiarly intense
way. Insistently, like a drum beat in the background of the novel,
runs the question: 'What is, what ought to be, what can be, the
most vital relation between man and woman?' At some points

there is a touching innocence in the way Paul and Miriam behave to each other; there are idyllic moments, when each uses the other as a means of exploring the possibilities of a beckoning future in terms not so much of education and intellectual ambition (though that does loom largely too) as of emotional fulfilment. The moments of tension, of frustration and misunderstanding and failure, are complicated by suggestions of a Lawrentian doctrine which seems to have been applied retroactively to a situation that has its own kind of poignant clarity without it. The touch of muddiness, the intrusive murk, which enters at some point into all Lawrence's greatest novels is not altogether absent here. What is it that happens? Does something deflect the fictional imagination as it seeks the objective correlative of its vision so that it veers momentarily off its true course? Or is it, as we have suggested, doubt, a certain uneasiness about the rightness and wholeness of this part of the action? *Sons and Lovers* is a book about modern civilization as well as about forms and perversions of love. Indeed, all Lawrence's novels are about modern civilization (and of course about other things as well). But for Lawrence problems of civilization must always be focused through problems of personal relationships, for civilization is judged by the kinds and qualities of human relationships it makes possible. It is perhaps an oversimplification but it is not wholly untrue to say that when Lawrence, in the midst of handling a situation dealing with personal relations, becomes too conscious of the fact that he is projecting through this personal situation some central truth about the nature of modern civilization, he is overcome by his responsibility and adds a dimension of eloquence or excessive symbolism that distorts his original vision. There is little enough of this in *Sons and Lovers*, which is in any case the most traditional of Lawrence's important novels, the only one in which he is content to write the novel more or less in conformity with the expectations of the intelligent novel-reader of the time. But it is not merely hindsight that makes us feel that there are elements in the novel which point outside the conventional use of the novel altogether. Even the use of physical description – of houses, rooms, fields, farms, landscape, physical objects of all kinds – is different from the use of description as background and setting in conventional novels of the time: things have an intensity which makes them vehicles for emotional comment or symbolic counterparts to characters and actions. And even incidents which in a more conventional novelist would be used merely to illustrate the kind of life that is here being presented – a miner's back being washed (a favourite symbolic incident of Lawrence's), animals in a barn – have a lyrical passion about them which links them immediately with the total line of meaning established by the novel. It was in developing this sort of thing much further that Lawrence was to make his characteristic contribution to the novel form.

*Eliseo Vivas*

# THE TRIUMPH OF ART (1960)

It is well known that *Sons and Lovers* attempts to elucidate the triangular relationship between Paul, his mother, and Miriam. If Paul's interest in literature and in painting comes into the picture, it is not because Lawrence, like Joyce, is centrally interested in giving us the portrait of the development of an artist. And if the relationship between the parents is accented, it is in order to give us the background out of which the triangular relationship grew. Lawrence wants to show how Paul and his mother were forced to come together because Gertrude's husband, the uncouth, drinking, bullying miner, was no husband to her nor was he, properly speaking, a father to his children.

Lawrence's gift as a writer, the living quality of his scenes, enable him almost to get away with his intention and to write off the father and the sweetheart. But he did not altogether succeed in doing so. And the novel shows the novelist to be not only a dribbling liar but in some respects, and in spite of his magnificent capacity to see, almost altogether blind. In *Sons and Lovers* Lawrence's intention and the intention of the novel are disparate. But I should add that in this case, the disparity does not constitute an artistic defect; it merely gives the novel qualities that Lawrence did not see were there, and that, within my knowledge, have not been generally noticed.

For Lawrence wants us to believe that both Paul's father and his sweetheart were at fault, and that his mother, Gertrude Morel, was a superior person, who rose above her miserable world by virtue of superiority of class and personal endowment, a loving mother and a wife made unhappy by an uncouth, drinking, irresponsible husband. But in terms of the evidence to be found in the novel, was this actually the case? There is no question that

Morel was not the right man for Gertrude, but was Gertrude the right wife for the miner?

Take the early scene in which Mrs Morel comes downstairs to find William shorn of 'the twining wisp of hair clustering around his head'. Mrs Morel is furious and with gripped, lifted fists, comes forward. Morel shrinks back. 'I could kill you, I could!' she says. She cries and later she tells her husband she has been silly. But we are told that 'she knew, and Morel knew, that the act had caused something momentous to take place in her soul. She remembered the scene all her life, as one in which she had suffered the most intensely.' And Lawrence goes on in the next paragraph: 'This act of masculine clumsiness was the spear through the side of her love for Morel. Before, while she had striven against him bitterly, she had fretted after him, as if he had gone astray from her. Now she ceased to fret for his love: he was an outsider to her. This made life much more bearable' (ch. 1). But this is belied by her reaction when she saw William's head shorn. She 'looked down at the jagged, close-clipped head of her child. . . . "Oh – my boy!" she faltered.' But before he cut his son's curls Morel was already an outsider. And because without asking her the man had clipped her boy's curls, she would remember the scene all her life. All one can say, confronted with the writer's statement, is that whether he knew it or not, he was giving us a vivid and living picture of a woman who had an unusual capacity to nurse a slight injury and had a powerful capacity for resentment. But does the writer know what he is presenting us with? Since the novel gives the writer the lie, the answer must be that he does and he does not. And we are here faced, not with a contradiction, but with a psychological conflict.

In any case, Paul's mother-sweetheart is a hard woman, a willful, unbending woman, and Paul is a myopic, love-blinded boy and young man. She would reform the miner she married, she would bring him up to her level of manners and gentility, and when it becomes clear to her that her husband cannot be reformed and when the physical attraction that brought them together subsides, she begins a relentless, ruthless war against him, setting the children against their father. The reason for her attitude is that he bullied them and drank: 'The sense of his sitting in all his pit-dirt, drinking after a long day's work . . . made Mrs Morel unable to bear herself. From her the feeling was transmitted to the other children. She never suffered alone any more: the children suffered with her' (ch. iv). But Mrs Morel was more than a willful, unbending woman. Paul, in the entanglement of an Oedipal relationship, could not see it, and Lawrence gives no indication that he sees it, but Mrs Morel was not a good mother to Paul and while Lawrence did in fact try to hand Paul's mother 'the laurels of victory', as Jessie Chambers points out, and while Miriam was indeed defeated and cast off, the price was high. We do not know what happens to Paul when he reaches the city towards which he turns at the end of the book. But we know that the struggle has turned him already into a cruel man and has damaged his capacity for normal sexual relations.

With cruelty goes pathos. For the reader who reads it with care the book is instinct with desolating pathos, when he considers the illusions in which Mrs Morel and her children live. The belief in the mother's superiority because she comes from a class just a notch higher than her husband, the belief that theirs is a home superior to their neighbors' because, living in a corner house, they pay a few more pennies for it than their neighbors do, the belief that they have better taste and superior education (which they do have, but which makes them pitiful snobs) – the hollowness of their values is pathetic. And Lawrence does not see their pathos. Neither through irony nor by any other means does he give us an indication that he sees through Gertrude Morel and her children. He is utterly lucid about the miner's faults. But about Paul's and his mother's false values he is blind.

How do we know about Paul's cruelty? We know from his treatment of his sweetheart. It is true that there is an important extenuating circumstance. The love between Paul and Miriam developed so slowly and so unconsciously, that by the time Paul realized clearly that Miriam could not satisfy his sexual needs, the involvement between them could only be severed by brutal surgery; there was no other way. When Miriam was twenty-one, Paul wrote to her that she was a nun and reproached her because in all their relations the body did not enter. After this letter was sent we are told that Paul, then twenty-three, was still a virgin, and that this was the end of the first phase of Paul's love-affair with Miriam. One can hardly blame Paul for discovering that what he needed was, in Miriam's words, 'a sort of baptism of fire in passion' (ch. XII). But while it is not necessary to take the attitude of a judge, and while in any case passing moral judgments on characters in books is an act of supererogation which interferes with the revelation the artist seeks to make, we cannot overlook the fact that Paul was cruel and that he knew it. Lawrence tells us that Paul 'fought against his mother almost as he fought against Miriam' (ch. IX). But this statement we may disregard, for the evidence of the novel gives it the lie. He did not fight against his mother; he grew in bondage and until her death in bondage he remained. And while his mother did not fear Clara and did not interfere with his affair with her, she resented Miriam bitterly and she did not interfere when her son-lover was unspeakably cruel towards his sweetheart. His cruelty was part of the fruits of her victory.

We know that the struggle damaged Paul's capacity for normal sexual relations from the account of Paul's affair with Clara Dawes. For a brief moment the affair appeared to be satisfactory. On one occasion at least it led to an experience the depth and amplitude of which was what Paul had yearned for and Miriam had not been able to provide. But the affair soon peters out and Paul ends up by virtually making Clara return to her husband. What is wrong between Paul and Clara? The book does not reveal the cause and therefore we cannot answer the question. But the fact that the book does not reveal it is itself significant. For a time Clara gives Paul what Miriam could not give him, the complete erotic satisfaction he had long craved. While the pee-wits scream in the field, they come together in an embrace of love and both seem to achieve complete fulfillment. 'They had met, and included in their meeting the thrust of the manifold grass-stems, the cry of the peewit and the wheel of the stars' (ch. XIII). Which is to say that the universe has been involved in their love, and this is as it should be. And not more than three lines later we are told, 'And after such an evening they both were very still, having known the immensity of passion.' But if they *both* had known the immensity of passion, why had the passion, as we are told only a little over a dozen pages later, 'failed her often'? And what prevents them from reaching again the height of that one time when the peewits had called? And why does Paul finally hand Clara back to Dawes? Surely this is a question in which we are legitimately interested and to which we need an answer. The failure to give an answer leaves us in the dark about the relationship between Clara and Paul. What went wrong between them? For a man who has had a sexual experience with a woman as complete and deep as that which Paul had with Clara, and who had wanted just that kind of experience, would not give the woman up as easily as Paul did. But the point I wish to make is not that Paul handed Clara back to her husband, but that the action is not grounded in anything that happens to them. We are left here with an unanswered question that the story itself gives rise to, not one we introduced from the outside.

This is not the only piece of evidence we have of Paul's incapacity for the complete sexual experience for which he craves. There is something else in the account of the affair between Paul and Clara that we must examine. On the occasion already mentioned we are told that the experience constituted for both a complete and deep consummation. But why then did the experience fail to be the first cause of the ripening of the bond between them? The universe was involved in their affair the evening the peewits were screaming in the field. This is as it should be: they are part of the earth, and at the moment of love-death, the earth and the stars are part of their experience. After the evening Paul and Clara are still, having known 'the immensity of passion'. But the experience does not lead to tenderness between them. The fierceness, the wildness, the naked hunger are appeased and we are told that 'in the morning Paul had considerable peace and was happy in himself'. This sentence suggests a kind of emotional solipsism which neither Paul nor Clara broke out of during their liaison. Even at the time he was most completely satisfied by her, Paul's mode of being is that of aloneness.

Sexual completion is no bridge thrown across from one self to the other, to bring them together in tenderness, mutual dependence, and understanding. The morning after the evening when the peewits screamed in the field, we are told that 'the intensity of passion began to burn him again', and of Clara we are told that she 'was mad with desire of him' (ch. XIII). But each seems to be, for the other, a mere means to an end, and when the end is achieved, it is enjoyed in isolation.

*Maurice Beebe*

# THE ARTIST THEME (1964)

LAWRENCE'S insistence on art as experience, a corollary of which is his likening of the artistic process to the sex act, puts him in the tradition of those writers who feel that the richness of a work of art may be measured by the completeness and intensity of the felt life manifested in the work. Believing this, Lawrence was eager to recruit the assistance of those who had shared his experiences, as when he drew upon Jessie Chambers and Frieda Lawrence for the writing of *Sons and Lovers*. The more viewpoints represented in the work, the more felt life. 'Form for him', Graham Hough has written, 'was the embodiment of an experience, and a form not lived through in experience was impossible to him.'[1] This conception of art places Lawrence outside the tradition represented by such writers as James, Flaubert, and Joyce, writers who held that the artist must remain detached from life in order to see it clearly and who produced static works of art dealing often, it is true, with personal experience, but experience somehow finished, exhausted, and thus subject to the artist's deliberate control and manipulation. Lawrence's art is more kinetic; the experience is lived in the process of writing as Lawrence, like Melville in *Moby Dick*, explores a situation which he does not fully understand. The poem or novel becomes a purgation and works out its fulfillment, so that the artist is liberated from *that* experience and released for others which, in turn, will be lived through both progressively and destructively until they also are turned into art. Each successful work of art – like each successful sexual union, Lawrence would say – represents a creative renewal.

In the final version of *Sons and Lovers* the artist theme is scarcely the dominant one. Paul Morel's relationship to himself and his art is less apparent to the reader than his relationship to the women in his life, his mother, Miriam Leivers, and Clara Dawes. Presumably the two earlier versions of the novel (which Lawrence called 'Paul Morel') were closer to the *Bildungsroman* tradition than is the finished version, and it is probable that in the early drafts Paul's development as an artist received more emphasis. Perhaps because Frieda Lawrence's enthusiastic adoption of Freudian theory helped Lawrence to alter the emphasis from Paul as an individual to his representative role as son and lover, the artist theme tends to be subordinated. Nonetheless, an understanding of the artist theme helps to clear up some of the mysteries of the novel which have not yet been satisfactorily explained by the more obvious themes.

These themes are identified in Lawrence's letter to Edward Garnett, and no interpretation of *Sons and Lovers* can afford to ignore the author's own statement of intention:

It follows this idea: a woman of character and refinement goes into the lower class, and has no satisfaction in her own life. She has had a passion for her husband, so the children are born of passion, and have heaps of vitality. But as her sons grow up she selects them as lovers – first the eldest, then the second. These sons are *urged* into life by their reciprocal love of their mother – urged on and on. But when they come to manhood, they can't love, because their mother is the strongest power of their lives, and holds them. . . . As soon as the young men come into contact with women, there's a split. William gives his sex to a fribble, and his mother holds his soul. But the split kills him, because he doesn't know where he is. The next son gets a woman who fights for his soul – fights his mother. The son loves the mother – all the sons hate and are jealous of the father. The battle goes on between the mother and the girl, with the son as object. The mother gradually proves stronger, because of the tie of blood. The son decides to leave his soul in his mother's hands, and, like his elder brother, go for passion. He gets passion. Then the split begins to tell again. But, almost unconsciously, the mother realizes what is the matter, and begins to die. The son casts off his mistress, attends to his mother dying. He is left in the end naked of everything, with the drift towards death.

Two related themes are suggested by Lawrence's précis. The dominant one is that of the Oedipus complex. This leads to Paul's repression, an aspect of which is the second theme: loving his mother too deeply, Paul cannot get body and soul together in his relations with other women. Therefore, Paul is 'split', and the novel itself, according to Mark Schorer,[2] is also split between the sections describing Paul's love of his mother and those describing his relations with Miriam and Clara. I believe that the stalemate between these two themes is ultimately overcome through the emergence of a third theme: the liberating force of artistic creativity. Unless there is some such resolving theme, we would have to agree with Schorer that the novel is split not only between intention and performance, but also between idea and form, and we should have to agree in turn with those critics who feel that the last part of the novel is a failure.

As many commentators have pointed out, Lawrence's account of the novel is an unreliable description of the story we read. If the book ended with the death of the mother and the defeat of Paul, the formula would work generally if not in all details. However, Paul is eventually regenerated and, far from drifting toward death – at least in its conventional meaning – seems at the end of the story to be liberated and redeemed so that he can move on to life. The obvious inadequacy of Lawrence's understanding of the book he had written lends support to the view that *Sons and Lovers* contains a buried theme that enabled Lawrence subconsciously to resolve conflicts which are unsolvable on the conscious level. Paul is once described as 'producing good stuff without knowing what he was doing'. So with Lawrence.

It seems to me apparent that neither the Freudian reading nor one which emphasizes the concept of a split answers some of the questions raised by a close reading of the novel. If it is intended to illustrate the case of a young man defeated by an Oedipus complex, how do we explain the fact that Paul becomes a friend and protector of the father-surrogate, Baxter Dawes, that he deliberately kills his mother, or that, with Clara at any rate, there is little evidence of sexual inhibition? Similarly, if we see the

novel primarily in terms of the 'split' theme, which would have
Clara represent physical love and Miriam cerebral love, how do
we justify the befogging of this theme through Paul's physical
intimacy with Miriam? Mark Spilka asks another key question –
who defeats Miriam and Clara? – and answers it by saying not
the mother, as the Freudian commentators would have it, but
their own inadequacies.[3] Just as important, I would say, is that
hard core of aloneness in Paul which none of his women can share.

Paul Morel is sensitive, shy, and introverted – traits associated
with the stereotype of the artistic temperament. He is an intent
observer of things, and has the 'impersonal, deliberate gaze of an
artist'. He has the faculty of concentrating on his work to the
exclusion of everything around him; and though he has misgivings about everything else, 'he believed firmly in his work,
that it was good and valuable. In spite of fits of depression,
shrinking, everything, he believed in his work.' That, however
little we may hear, directly of his art in *Sons and Lovers*, Paul
Morel is clearly a true artist is shown not only by such internal
evidence, but also by the fact that to the extent any fictional
character may be equated with its living model, Paul is a self-
portrait of Lawrence. We are told that Paul 'loved to paint
large figures full of light, but not merely made up of lights and
cast shadows, like the impressionists; rather definite figures
that had a certain luminous quality, like some of Michael Angelo's
people. And these he fitted into a landscape, in what he thought
true proportion. He worked a great deal from memory, using
everybody he knew' (ch. XII). This description of Paul's art – one
of the few given in the novel – would apply to Lawrence's fiction
as well as his painting. Paul is supposed to be a painter, not a
writer, but in one passage Lawrence makes a telling slip: 'Often
he could not go on with his work. The pen stopped writing.'*

Paul has innately the temperament and the talent that are the
essential qualities of the artist. However, these are not enough in
themselves. The artist-to-be must also be motivated. The artist
theme blends with the Oedipus theme when we are told that
Paul's first motivation was simply his desire to please his mother:

* In its context (ch. xv) this seems to refer to Paul's *job* (as a clerk). G.S.

'When she was quiet so, she looked brave and rich with life, but as if she had been done out of her rights. It hurt the boy keenly, this feeling about her that she had never had her life's fulfillment: and his own incapability to make up to her hurt him with a sense of impotence, yet made him patiently dogged inside. It was his childish aim' (ch. IV). Gift offerings to the mother-queen Gertrude provide a running motif throughout the novel. In the climax of the first scene, William's gift of two egg cups, a feminine symbol as the Freudian interpreters make clear, is received gratefully, while the father's gift of a coconut, 'a hairy object', is accepted begrudgingly: ' "A man will part with anything so long as he's drunk," said Mrs Morel.' Later William brings his athletic trophies to his mother, like a knight to his lady, and Paul offers her his early drawings, like a court painter offering pictures to his queen. When Paul wins two first prizes in an exhibition, his mother is as exultant as if she had herself produced them: 'Paul was going to distinguish himself. She had a great belief in him, the more because he was unaware of his own powers. There was so much to come out of him. . . . She was to see herself fulfilled. Not for nothing had been her struggle' (ch. VII). Even at the end of the novel, when Paul is fighting against the despair caused by his mother's death, his justification for going on by painting or by begetting children is that 'they both carry on her effort'.

The struggle between Gertrude Morel and Miriam Leivers is not simply the vying of two women for Paul's love, but the jealous struggle of two patronesses for the homage of the artist and the right to control him. Miriam, in fact, often seems to be a muse – a 'shy, wild, quiveringly sensitive thing' who 'always looked so lost and out of place among people'. No wonder then that Paul thinks that 'she could scarcely stand the shock of physical love, even a passionate kiss'. Yet, because for Lawrence the artist's muse cannot be dissociated from his sexuality, Paul uses Miriam to bring forth his art in a way that Lawrence describes in obviously sexual terms: 'There was for him the most intense pleasure in talking about his work to Miriam. All his passion, all his wild blood, went into this intercourse with her, when he talked and conceived his work. She brought forth to him his imaginations. She did not understand, any more than a woman understands when she conceives a child in her womb' (ch. VIII). In view of this, it is not surprising that Paul's possessing her physically should become a dramatic necessity for the novel. Only then does Paul realize that even as muse she is false. She gives herself to him as a kind of sacrifice, but her aim is to possess by giving, without realizing that she must either keep her distance like a true muse or really be sacrificed if Paul is to move from one phase of his artistic development to another. She is 'always most interested in him as he appeared in his work' and essentially indifferent to him physically. Like his mother, therefore, she is not jealous of Clara Dawes, for she thinks that after Paul has 'achieved his baptism of fire in passion', he will return to her, 'for he would want to be owned, so that he could work'. Like his mother, too, she is not repudiated even after she has been sacrificed, for she has become assimilated into Paul and made use of, just as Jessie Chambers, by her own account, was used, then sacrificed for the writing of *Sons and Lovers*.[4] In keeping with Miriam's function as muse, it is her visit to Paul's apartment in the last chapter which reawakens his interest in his art and enables him to realize that 'work *can* be nearly everything to a man'.

Clara Dawes has happened to Paul in the meantime, and if the main trouble with Miriam is that 'she could not take him and relieve him of the responsibility of himself', it is partly because Paul has already discovered through Clara the liberating force which frees him from himself at the very moment when he becomes self-fulfilled. Clara, too, is presented in symbolic terms: she is Big Blonde Woman, sensuous and coarse, yet – as befits the mother-surrogate in the novel, also withdrawn and dignified. If she is a queen mother, she is also a Molly Bloom or a Eula Varner, and the contradictions in her make-up are those that we expect to find in the earth-moon-sea goddess who appears in so many guises throughout literature. Whereas Paul first possesses Miriam in bed, he takes Clara on the ground, after a compulsive, symbolic ordeal which brings them from the highway down a difficult riverbank so that their first physical intimacy may occur as close to the river as possible. Clara is associated with water – like the girl standing in mid-stream at the moment of consternation in Joyce's *Portrait of the Artist* – and the strongest image of Clara is when she stands naked and outlined against the immensity of the sea. But when, in this moment of realization, the moon disappears and Paul sees her 'dazzled out of sight by the sunshine', she appears to grow smaller, to change from sea goddess to mere woman to 'just a concentrated speck blown along, a tiny white foam-bubble, almost nothing among the morning', and it is at this moment that Paul realizes that he no longer needs her.

Because of Paul's Oedipal situation, he can be liberated and fulfilled, made whole as a man, only through a full sexual initiation. To the extent that Clara, like Miriam, is a surrogate for Paul's mother, Paul's intimacy with Clara carries overtones of incest and thus follows closely the archetypal 'solution' to the Oedipal situation in literature.[5] Whereas with Miriam in the sex act, Paul remained self-conscious, fumbling, guilt-stricken – partly at least because the similarity between Miriam and his mother was apparent to him – with Clara he finds himself carried away from self through passion. Lawrence's description of the sex act sounds like accounts by poets of the creative process in moments of true inspiration when the afflatus descends upon the artist and carries him along in spite of himself:

As a rule, when he started love-making, the emotion was strong enough to carry with it everything – reason, soul, blood – in a great sweep, like the Trent carries bodily its back-swirls and intertwinings, noiselessly. Gradually, the little criticisms, the little sensations, were lost, thought also went, everything borne along in one flood. He became, not a man with a mind, but a great instinct. His hands were like creatures, living; his limbs, his body, were all life and consciousness, subject to no will of his, but living in themselves. Just as he was, so it seemed the vigorous, wintry stars were strong also with life. He and they struck with the same pulse of fire, and the same joy of strength which held the bracken-frond stiff near his eyes held his own body firm. It was as if he, and the stars, and the dark herbage, and Clara were licked up in an immense tongue of flame, which tore onwards and upwards. Everything rushed along in living beside him; everything was still, perfect in itself, along with him. This wonderful stillness in each thing in itself, while it was being borne along in a very ecstasy of living, seemed the highest point of bliss. (ch. XIII)

Just as inspiration comes to the artist involuntarily and cannot be forced, so Paul and Clara discover that their lovemaking becomes less satisfactory when they experiment in an attempt to bring back lost glamor: 'And afterwards each of them was rather ashamed, and these things caused a distance between the two of them.'

Ultimately, though, Paul and Clara draw apart simply because she demands too much of him. She wants to love all the time – during the day, in broad sunlight, at work – whereas Paul is for Lawrence typically masculine in that he is interested in love only sporadically, taking the conventional view that there is a right time and place for everything. For man, Lawrence implies, sex is not the end, but a means. According to Frederick Hoffman's synopsis of Lawrence's philosophy of sex, 'man should go beyond the crucial union of egos which is the act of coition. For him it is the source of renewal, which should serve to drive him forward into creative group life. Woman offers the nucleus of further renewal, and supplements her husband's life by turning him back from time to time to the fountain source of his strength.'[6] The battle between the sexes is largely the result of this fundamental difference, for with woman love is the center of life; the creative act; for men it is only a bridge to creation. Thus Paul lectures Miriam:

'A woman only works with a part of herself. The real and vital part is covered up.'
'But a man can give *all* himself to a work?' she asked.
'Yes, practically.'
'And a woman only the unimportant part of herself?'
'That's it.'

The trouble with Miriam is that as an intellectual she would deny this –

She looked up at him, and her eyes dilated with anger. 'Then,' she said, 'if it's true, it's a great shame.' (ch. XV)

Clara, on the other hand, exults in her womanhood and offers Paul the dignity of a man–woman struggle as she strives to possess him completely and he fights to retain his independence. Because they are opposites, his satisfactory unions with her resolve all differences and give him a feeling of wholeness, of utter stasis in the midst of movement, if only momentarily.

Whereas Clara offers Paul the chance for a genuine struggle for dominance between a man and a woman, both his mother and Miriam assume that he 'would want to be owned so that he could work'. What they fail to realize is that there is a side to Paul which can never be owned – that side which shows itself in those moments of work when he is abstracted, 'producing good stuff without knowing what he was doing'. Even while his mother lies dying, he finds it possible to abstract himself and to work on his pictures, oblivious to all around him. This trait also parallels the successful lovemaking, for when Clara protests,

> 'But you've never given me yourself.'
> He knitted his brows angrily.
> 'If I start to make love to you,' he said, 'I just go like a leaf down the wind.'
> 'And leave me out of the count,' she said. (ch. XIII)

In this inability to give himself completely, Paul is very much like Aaron Sisson of *Aaron's Rod*, and the later novel deals openly with an aspect of Lawrence's character that is only dimly presented in *Sons and Lovers*. Aaron has 'a hard, opposing core in him', and 'his very being pivoted on the fact of his isolate self-responsibility, aloneness'. Thus: 'He never gave himself. He never came to her, *really*. He withheld himself. Yes, in those supreme and sacred times which for her were the whole culmination of life and being, the ecstasy of unspeakable passional conjunction, he was not really hers. He was withheld. He withheld the central core of himself, like the devil and hell-fiend he was. He cheated and made play with her tremendous passional soul, her sacred sex passion, most sacred of all things for a woman. All the time, some central part of him stood apart from her, aside, looking on.' Aaron, too, is an artist, and his flute, with its obvious phallic connotation, is not only the means of his art, but also a symbol of his aloneness. It is significant that Lawrence represents art by means of a strongly masculine symbol, for it is only such a conjunction that enables us to understand the leading thesis in *Sons and Lovers* that a man's work, his art, is something that can never be fully shared with women.

In the typical portrait-of-the-artist novel, the hero, blessed from the beginning with talent and the right temperament, becomes motivated through allegiance to some kind of 'master', often represented by a father, mother, or lover, then after a period of apprenticeship involving commitment to the standards of his chosen master finds it necessary to break away in order to become master in his own right. I have pointed out that Paul has the talent and temperament of the true artist and that he is motivated through a mother-worship represented dramatically in terms of his relations with the two mother-surrogates, Miriam and Clara. It remains necessary to consider the process of liberation.

In his phase of apprenticeship, Paul tries to deny the existence in himself of the qualities which he associates with his father. Walter Morel, for all his apparent sociability, is 'an outsider', thoroughly masculine in his interests and abilities. A good workman and skillful craftsman who sings when absorbed in his work, he too is an incipient artist, the best dancer in the village and once master of a dancing school. He breaks away from his wife, in much the same fashion and for basically the same reasons as did Aaron Sisson, for he too has a hard core of aloneness and finds it impossible to submit to his wife's domination. His realm is the black pit of the mine, and throughout the novel he is associated symbolically with the forces of night and darkness. Just as Aaron is compared to 'the devil and hell-fiend', so Walter Morel 'had denied the God in him'.

Paul begins to free himself from the oppression of his mother when he assumes the role of the father. Thus when he makes love to Clara he reverts unconsciously to the speech of Walter Morel. But the return of the father is best represented in terms of Paul's relationship with Baxter Dawes, Clara's estranged husband. As Daniel Weiss has pointed out, Baxter is physically similar to

Walter Morel and, like him, works with his hands and is the rejected husband of an educated woman.[7] In the beginning there is natural hostility between Baxter and Paul, similar to that between Paul and his father, but whereas the physical fights which threaten to occur between Paul (and William) with the father are always stopped by the mother's intervention, Paul and Baxter finally come together in actual battle. Significantly, the fight takes place at night, in mine-like darkness, and there can be little doubt that it is seen by Lawrence as a symbolic ordeal by which Paul proves his masculinity, even though in suddenly submitting to the other man and taking a beating he does so unconventionally. The growing friendship between Paul and Baxter after the fight is less mysterious than it seems on the surface, for now the two men are more alike than different. To some extent, Paul shares Baxter's illness and recuperation – traditional symbols of death and rebirth in the *Bildungsroman*. Finally, Paul, who already realizes that Clara is a bridge for him rather than his goal, engineers a reconciliation between Clara and Baxter. If Gertrude Morel suggests Hamlet's mother, so Paul is like Hamlet in that he stages a drama, with Clara and Baxter as player-queen and player-king, that represents his own internal conflict. When he plays thus the artist, he is already a long way on the road to emancipation. He has admitted the father in himself.

It remains necessary for Paul to destroy his dead self. This, I think, is represented in the novel by Mrs Morel's death. Paul kills his mother by giving her an overdose of medicine. The ethics of euthanasia aside, this form of death is not dramatically necessary in the novel; in fact, if the novel were intended only to show the defeat of Paul, it would be better for Mrs Morel simply to die. Instead, she clings desperately to life, fearing to the end the forces of darkness. The conflict of man-will and woman-will culminates in Paul's giving her – fitting climax to the gift-offering motif in the novel – the bitter cup of poison which kills her and a part of himself, but which frees him for a new life.

After the death of Mrs Morel, it is natural that Paul should undergo a period of despair in which the feeling of emptiness which engulfs him is so strong that he ceases even to practice his art. He is derelict now, truly alienated in that he feels a barrier between himself and the life around him: 'He could not get in touch.' Like his father, he too is now an outsider. But this is a period of symbolic death for Paul, necessary if he is to be liberated from the restrictions of his apprenticeship, and he waits to be reborn into a new life. The visit from Miriam makes him realize that the past which she represents is now dead for him – 'and they went out talking together, he talking, she feeling dead'. After he has left her, however, he suddenly experiences a moment of consecration very similar to that experienced by Stephen Dedalus in Joyce's *Portrait*:

Whatever spot he stood on, there he stood alone. From his breast, from his mouth, sprang the endless space, and it was there behind him, everywhere. The people hurrying along the streets offered no obstruction to the void in which he found himself. They were small shadows whose footsteps and voices could be heard, but in each of them the same night, the same silence. He got off the car. In the country all was dead still. Little stars shone high up; little stars spread far away in the flood-waters, a firmament below. Everywhere the vastness and terror of the immense night which is roused and stirred for a brief while by the day, but which returns, and will remain at last eternal, holding everything in its silence and its living gloom. There was no Time, only Space. . . . On every side the immense dark silence seemed pressing him, so tiny a spark, into extinction, and yet, almost nothing, he could not be extinct. Night, in which everything was lost, went reaching out, beyond stars and sun. Stars and sun, a few bright grains, went spinning round for terror, and holding each other in embrace, there in a darkness that outpassed them all, and left them tiny and daunted. So much, and himself, infinitesimal, at the core a nothingness, and yet not nothing. (ch.xv)

Stephen Dedalus and Paul share in their moments of baptismal consecration the feeling of complete aloneness, the sensation that they are outside time, and the awareness of perfect stasis even in the midst of movement. Stephen, though, almost immediately feels triumphant. With Paul there is as much terror as triumph. Twice he whimpers 'Mother!', then suddenly knows that 'she was gone, intermingled herself'. The novel concludes: 'But no, he would not give in. Turning sharply, he walked towards the city's gold phosphorescence. His fists were shut, his mouth set fast. He would not take that direction, to the darkness, to follow her. He walked towards the faintly humming, glowing town, quickly.' The ending is ambiguous, though most readers would agree that it appears to be more affirmative than negative. He will not follow his mother into death, though if Lawrence really meant to leave him 'with the drift towards death', as he wrote to Garnett, he must have meant that Paul cannot leave his mother entirely behind, that he and she and everything are now 'intermingled' and that he carries this realization into a new phase of life.[8] If 'quickly' suggests life (the quick and the dead), as Harry Moore has argued,[9] Paul is committing himself to the 'faintly humming, glowing town' just as Stephen shouts 'Welcome, O life' at the same time as he rejects the dead life of his past. Joyce's description of Stephen at the moment of consecration – 'His soul had arisen from the grave of boyhood, spurning her grave-clothes'[10] – could apply to Paul as well. Both Joyce and Lawrence conclude their portraits of the artist with the heroes, having tested and found wanting the claims of love and family, poised for exile, but an exile which is to lead to creative renewal.

Seymour Betsky has said that '*Sons and Lovers* is a purgation become the successful work of art.'[11] The novel itself thus stands for the transformation of life into art. Lawrence has tapped the Sacred Fount and used up the life which finds its way into the novel. Having done so, he, like Paul, is both dead and reborn. Lawrence's next novel, *The Rainbow*, reveals a new and different Lawrence, though it is the same Lawrence too in that the author of *Sons and Lovers*, having lived through that experience and killed it by transforming it into art, is now 'intermingled' – like Paul's murdered mother.

## NOTES

1. *The Dark Sun: A Study of D. H. Lawrence* (New York, 1957) p. 41.
2. See the essay on pp. 106–11 of the present volume. G.S.

3. *The Love Ethic of D. H. Lawrence* (Bloomington, 1955) p. 74.

4. *D. H. Lawrence: A Personal Record* (1935). [See the extract reprinted in the present volume on p. 41. G.S.]

5. See William Wasserstrom, 'In Gertrude's Closet', in *Yale Review*, XLVIII (Winter 1959) 245–65.

6. F. Hoffman, *Freudianism and the Literary Mind* (Baton Rouge, 1945).

7. 'Oedipus in Nottingham', in *Literature and Psychology*, VII (Aug. 1957) 36. [Included in a book with this title, New York, 1962. G.S.]

8. Lawrence's poem 'The Virgin Mother' would seem to substantiate this interpretation. See *Complete Poems* (1957) I 83–5.

9. *The Life and Works of D. H. Lawrence* (New York, 1951) p. 105.

10. *A Portrait of the Artist as a Young Man* (New York, 1928) p. 197.

11. 'Rhythm and Theme: D. H. Lawrence's *Sons and Lovers*', in *The Achievement of D. H. Lawrence*, ed. F. J. Hoffman and H. T. Moore (1953) p. 143. [Reprinted in the present volume, pp. 130–43. G.S.]

# H. M. Daleski

# THE RELEASE: THE FIRST PERIOD (1965)

LAWRENCE's portrayal of Paul's relations with his father and mother has none of the distortion which weakens his representation of the marriage. To the extent that he is to be identified with Paul, he made it clear that the portrayal, among other things, was a deliberate self-purgation: 'I felt you had gone off from me a bit, because of *Sons and Lovers*', he wrote to a friend. 'But one sheds one's sicknesses in books – repeats and presents again one's emotions, to be master of them.'[1] From the outset he has a clear understanding of the nature of Paul's love for his mother and his hatred of his father.

Paul is early overwhelmed by the unnatural love which his mother fosters in him. When he is a young boy she accepts the flowers which he brings her like 'a woman accepting a love-token' (ch. IV); on the day that he goes for his interview at Jordan's she is gay with him, 'like a sweetheart' (ch. V), and they walk through the streets of Nottingham 'feeling the excitement of lovers having an adventure together' (ch. V); and, eventually, everything he does is 'for her' – 'the two shared lives' (ch. VI). As far as Paul's relations with his father are concerned, the boy is from infancy united with his mother against him. When Morel cuts his wife's forehead open with the drawer which he flings at her, it is Paul whom she is holding on her lap, and as she averts her face from Morel's stumbling concern, blood from the wound drips on to the baby's hair; Morel is sure that it soaks through to the scalp (ch. II). This additional, if symbolic, tie of blood which Paul shares with his mother in her withdrawal from Morel is set over and against his more matter-of-fact connection with his father. As he grows up Paul is convinced of his hatred for his father:

Paul hated his father. As a boy he had a fervent private religion. 'Make him stop drinking,' he prayed every night. 'Lord, let my father die,' he prayed very often. 'Let him not be killed at pit,' he prayed when, after tea, the father did not come home from work. (ch. IV)

This is a delightful example of childish inconsequence; it is also, despite the initial affirmation, indicative of Paul's ambivalence towards his father.

That Lawrence knows what is behind Paul's excessive feelings of love and hate is asserted by one of the subtlest scenes in the book:

He had taken off his collar and tie, and rose, bare-throated, to go to bed. As he stooped to kiss his mother, she threw her arms round his neck, hid her face on his shoulder, and cried, in a whimpering voice, so unlike her own that he writhed in agony: 'I can't bear it. I could let another woman – but not her. She'd leave me no room, not a bit of room –'
And immediately he hated Miriam bitterly.
'And I've never – you know, Paul – I've never had a husband – not really –'
He stroked his mother's hair, and his mouth was on her throat.
'And she exults so in taking you from me – she's not like ordinary girls.'
'Well, I don't love her, mother,' he murmured, bowing his head and hiding his eyes on her shoulder in misery. His mother kissed him a long, fervent kiss.
'My boy!' she said, in a voice trembling with passionate love.
Without knowing, he gently stroked her face.
'There,' said his mother, 'now go to bed. You'll be *so* tired in the morning.' As she was speaking she heard her husband coming. 'There's your father – now go.' Suddenly she looked at him almost as if in fear. 'Perhaps I'm selfish. If you want her, take her, my boy.' (ch. VIII)

Mrs Morel is pathetic in her jealousy of Miriam, but if Miriam is not like an ordinary girl she herself hardly behaves like an ordinary mother. Under the painful stimulus of her complaints about her husband, the love between mother and son takes on a dangerously erotic character. And Mrs Morel is at least partially aware of what she is doing: with the approach of her husband she realizes, with a sudden feeling of guilt, how she has compromised her son. But her recantation is of little avail in the face of Paul's aroused passion for her. His passion seeks an outlet, and balked in the direction it would take, it turns viciously on his father. When Morel comes in, he takes a pie which Mrs Morel has specially bought for Paul, and on being challenged by her, he flings it into the fire. He too is ready for violence, for he has not mistaken the import of the scene which meets him:

> Paul started to his feet.
> 'Waste your own stuff!' he cried.
> 'What – what!' suddenly shouted Morel, jumping up and clenching his fist. 'I'll show yer, yer young jockey!'
> 'All right!' said Paul viciously, putting his head on one side. 'Show me!'
> He would at that moment dearly have loved to have a smack at something. Morel was half crouching, fists up, ready to spring. The young man stood, smiling with his lips.
> 'Ussha!' hissed the father, swiping round with a great stroke just past his son's face. He dared not, even though so close, really touch the young man, but swerved an inch away.
> 'Right!' said Paul, his eyes upon the side of his father's mouth, where in another instant his fist would have hit. He ached for that stroke. But he heard a faint moan from behind. His mother was deadly pale and dark at the mouth. . . . (ch. VIII)

Paul desists, ostensibly for the sake of his mother, but within the wider context of the book as a whole it is significant that neither father nor son can actually bring himself to strike the other. Their enmity is real enough but it is the surface enmity of an unhealthy rivalry rather than that of a deep-seated personal antagonism:

> 'Can you go to bed, mother?'
> 'Yes, I'll come.'
> 'Sleep with Annie, mother, not with him.'
> 'No. I'll sleep in my own bed.'
> 'Don't sleep with him, mother.'
> 'I'll sleep in my own bed.' (ch. VIII)

The clash between Paul and Morel is of course a striking example of an Oedipal situation, and indeed on publication the book was treated as a *locus classicus* by early English Freudians.[2] 'Yes', Frieda wrote to Frederick J. Hoffman, 'Lawrence knew about Freud before he wrote the final draft of *Sons and Lovers*', but I am inclined to accept Hoffman's conclusion that 'it is doubtful . . . that the revision of *Sons and Lovers* was more than superficially affected by Lawrence's introduction to psycho-analysis'.[3] At that time Lawrence's knowledge of Freudian theory was derived at second-hand from Frieda, and she probably did no more than confirm his intuitive apprehension of the nature of Paul's relations with his parents. Nor does the book betray any signs of artificial grafting.

The sort of penetrative understanding which is at work behind the organization of the scene I have just discussed informs countless incidents in the book. There is, for instance, the scene when Paul is ill as a young boy:

On retiring to bed, the father would come into the sick-room. He was always very gentle if anyone were ill. But he disturbed the atmosphere for the boy.

'Are ter asleep, my darlin'?' Morel asked softly.

'No; is my mother comin'?'

'She's just finishin' foldin' the clothes. Do you want anything?' Morel rarely 'thee'd' his son.

'I don't want nothing. But how long will she be?'

'Not long, my duckie.'

The father waited undecidedly on the hearthrug for a moment or two. He felt his son did not want him. . . .

He loitered about indefinitely. The boy began to get feverish with irritation. His father's presence seemed to aggravate all his sick impatience. At last Morel, after having stood looking at his son awhile, said softly:

'Good-night, my darling.'

'Good-night,' Paul replied, turning round in relief to be alone.

Paul loved to sleep with his mother. Sleep is still most perfect, in spite of hygienists, when it is shared with a beloved. The warmth, the security and peace of soul, the utter comfort from the touch of the other, knits the sleep, so that it takes the body and soul completely in its healing. Paul lay against her and slept, and got better; whilst she, always a bad sleeper, fell later on into a profound sleep that seemed to give her faith. (ch. IV)

Morel, it is seen, does not have to be provocative to be rejected. Paul's rebuffing of his father's warm gentleness and kindliness is only understandable in terms of the inbred family situation; and indeed, as the concluding paragraph makes clear, the conflict between father and son which manifests itself later in an apparent readiness to come to blows is incipient here. At this stage Paul's childish desire to sleep with his mother is presented simply and naturally as a longing for maternal warmth and security, but later developments are anticipated in the ambiguous phraseology of the paragraph. We are reminded of Lawrence's claim in the well-known letter to Edward Garnett that the development of the book 'is slow, like growth'.[4] It is only by slow stages that Paul's incestuous love for his mother expresses itself in the frankly passionate kisses of his manhood: first, there is the seemingly childlike innocence of the foregoing scene; then there is the more open ambiguity of his attitude as a youth. Paul is sixteen when he falls seriously ill. It is a cruel irony that the love which then makes him desperately assert his will to live should later prove to be so deathly in its effects:

Paul was very ill. His mother lay in bed at nights with him; they could not afford a nurse. He grew worse, and the crisis approached. One night he tossed into consciousness in the ghastly, sickly feeling of dissolution, when all the cells in the body seem in intense irritability to be breaking down, and consciousness makes a last flare of struggle, like madness.

'I s'll die, mother!' he cried, heaving for breath on the pillow.

She lifted him up, crying in a small voice:

'Oh, my son – my son!'

That brought him to. He realized her. His whole will rose up and arrested him. He put his head on her breast, and took ease of her for love. (ch. VI)

The immediate effect of Mrs Morel's poisonously possessive love for Paul is her implacable hostility to Miriam. From the moment she senses his interest in the girl she tries to fight her off:

> Always when he went with Miriam, and it grew rather late, he knew his mother was fretting and getting angry about him – why, he could not understand. As he went into the house, flinging down his cap, his mother looked up at the clock. . . .
> 'She must be wonderfully fascinating, that you can't get away from her, but must go trailing eight miles at this time of night.'
> He was hurt between the past glamour with Miriam and the knowledge that his mother fretted. He had meant not to say anything, to refuse to answer. But he could not harden his heart to ignore his mother.
> 'I *do* like to talk to her,' he answered irritably.
> 'Is there nobody else to talk to?'
> 'You wouldn't say anything if I went with Edgar.'
> 'You know I should. You know, whoever you went with, I should say it was too far for you to go trailing, late at night, when you've been to Nottingham. Besides' – her voice suddenly flashed into anger and contempt – 'it is disgusting – bits of lads and girls courting.' (ch. VII)

Paul's inability to understand Mrs Morel's antagonism to Miriam is, at this stage of the narrative, bound up with his own repressions. Struggling as he is with his complex emotions towards his mother, it is hardly surprising he should fail to realize that her jealousy is almost nakedly sexual. The real reason for her annoyance is casually phrased as an afterthought, but her sudden violent employment of the word 'disgusting' and the illogical asperity of the comment itself are sure guides to her feeling. It is seldom, however, that the serpent in the garden slithers out of the undergrowth in this way; Mrs Morel effectively rationalizes her dislike of Miriam:

> 'She exults – she exults as she carries him off from me,' Mrs Morel cried in her heart when Paul had gone. 'She's not like an ordinary woman, who can leave me my share in him. She wants to absorb him. She wants to draw him out and absorb him till there is nothing left of him, even for himself. He will never be a man on his own feet – she will suck him up.' So the mother sat, and battled and brooded bitterly. (ch. VIII)

It is a further indication of Lawrence's comprehensive view –
I have already referred in this respect to his treatment of the
Morel marriage – that Mrs Morel's criticism of Miriam should
be just; but, as R. P. Draper has pointed out,[5] she does not
perceive its application to herself. It is she who is preventing
Paul from being a man on his own feet, and though she is not as
hostile to Clara as to Miriam, her carping at his attachment to
the married woman is parallel to her interference in his relationship with the girl. Her approval of her son's women is always
irremediably conditional: 'You know I should be *glad* [at your
association with Clara]', she tells Paul, 'if she weren't a married
woman' (ch. XII).

Since Paul cannot but agree with his mother's objections to
Miriam, it is her attitude to Clara which finally makes him aware
of her possessive jealousy. Mrs Morel, asking more of Paul than
he can give, relentlessly holding him back, plays the same part
as the 'beggar-woman' of 'End of Another Home Holiday':

> While ever at my side,
> Frail and sad, with grey, bowed head,
> The beggar-woman, the yearning-eyed
> Inexorable love goes lagging.

Eventually Paul comes to realize that his mother is defrauding
him of life:

> Then sometimes he hated her, and pulled at her bondage. His
> life wanted to free itself of her. It was like a circle where life
> turned back on itself, and got no farther. She bore him, loved him,
> kept him, and his love turned back into her, so that he could
> not be free to go forward with his own life, really love another
> woman. . . . (ch. XIII)

And from pulling at her bondage it is but a short step to a scarcely
disguised wish for her death:

> 'And as for wanting to marry,' said his mother, 'there's plenty
> of time yet.'
> 'But no, mother. I even love Clara, and I did Miriam; but to
> *give* myself to them in marriage I couldn't. I couldn't belong to
> them. They seem to want *me*, and I can't ever give it them.'

'You haven't met the right woman.'

'And I never shall meet the right woman while you live,' he said. (ch. XIII)

These two passages alone, quite apart from the circumstances of Mrs Morel's death which I shall discuss in a moment, should suffice to refute the criticism that in *Sons and Lovers* Lawrence capitulates to his mother. This misreading of the book derives, it would seem, from an uncritical acceptance of Jessie Chambers' verdict: 'His mother conquered indeed, but the vanquished one was her son. In *Sons and Lovers* Lawrence handed his mother the laurels of victory.' In her wake the froth gathers: '. . . at the same time that the book condemns the mother it justifies her',[6] '. . . the story of Paul Morel . . . was to be his mother's justification and apotheosis',[7] '. . . hence the distortion he made in the presentation of Miriam in his great novel, in order that the mother might triumph',[8] '. . . Lawrence was unable to detach himself from the mother whom he celebrates as heroine or to achieve the impersonality that the most personal art requires',[9] 'Lawrence tells us that Paul "fought against his mother almost as he fought against Miriam" (ch. IX). But this statement we may disregard, for the evidence of the novel gives it the lie. He did not fight against his mother; he grew in bondage and until her death in bondage he remained.'[10] It is necessary to clarify this assumption of the mother's triumph, for it underlies the even more widely accepted view that the Miriam section of the book (which remains to be discussed) is both false and a failure. Mrs Morel does have a limited triumph, in so far as Paul does not marry while she lives, but then his failure to do so is only partially attributable to her; it has as much to do with Miriam and Clara. The extent, moreover, to which Paul himself, because of his mother's influence, is to blame for the failure is fully and frankly indicated, as the two passages quoted above should make abundantly clear. And the so-called 'justification' of Mrs Morel is a matter not of approbation but of truly creative presentment of character, whereby the motivating circumstances of her overpowering love for Paul are sympathetically portrayed. They may even be shown as extenuating circumstances, but that her influence is crippling – it is the theme of the book – is quite unambiguous. If it is crippling, however, it is not paralysing – as Jessie Chambers apparently believed. Paul makes his own stand for life.

There is, significantly, an image associated with the idea of crippling in the poem 'Monologue of a Mother':

> Strange he is, my son, for whom I have waited like a lover;
> . . .
> Like a thin white bird blown out of the northern seas,
> Like a bird from the far north blown with a broken wing
> Into our sooty garden, he drags and beats
> Along the fence perpetually, seeking release
> From me, from the hand of my love which creeps up, needing
> His happiness, while he in displeasure retreats.

Like the son in the poem and like the bird with a broken wing, Paul also seeks release; and it is surely an Empsonian ambiguity that the chapter which describes the painful suffering and death of Mrs Morel should be entitled 'The Release'.

Any interpretation of *Sons and Lovers* must finally centre on this chapter, and so it is perhaps as well first to marshal the facts. Mrs Morel is stricken with cancer and her long-drawn-out suffering is so acute that Paul wishes she would die (ch. XIV). Weeks pass and he begins to dilute her milk so that it will not nourish her (ch. XIV). Finally, Paul decides to end her misery by giving her an overdose of morphia:

> That evening he got all the morphia pills there were, and took them downstairs. Carefully he crushed them to powder.
> 'What are you doing?' said Annie.
> 'I s'll put 'em in her night milk.'
> Then they both laughed together like two conspiring children. Ont op of all their horror flickered this little sanity. (ch. XIV)

Mrs Morel lasts through the night, and Paul wonders whether her 'horrible breathing' will stop if he piles 'heavy clothes on top of her' (ch. XIV). She dies the next morning.

Clearly, on one level, Paul's killing of his mother is a mercy-killing. His agony at her suffering is poignantly described, and

when she is dead he can only helplessly wish that she were alive
again:

> She lay like a maiden asleep. . . . She would wake up. She would
> lift her eyelids. She was with him still. He bent and kissed her
> passionately. But there was coldness against his mouth. He bit
> his lip with horror. Looking at her, he felt he could never, never
> let her go. No! He stroked the hair from her temples. That, too,
> was cold. He saw the mouth so dumb and wondering at the hurt.
> Then he crouched on the floor, whispering to her:
> 'Mother, mother!' (ch. XIV)

But, on a deeper level, the killing and the desire to smother his
mother have a significance which he is not aware of consciously.
I think we must concur with Anthony West and Graham Hough
that Paul's killing of his mother represents, symbolically, both
a repudiation of what she stands for[11] and a decisive act of self-
liberation,[12] as does his turning towards the city at the end of the
book:

> But no, he would not give in. Turning sharply, he walked
> towards the city's gold phosphorescence. His fists were shut, his
> mouth set fast. He would not take that direction, to the darkness,
> to follow her. He walked towards the faintly humming, glowing
> town, quickly.

I believe that a close textual analysis of the passage, quoted
above, which describes the preparation of the death-draught,
reveals further significances of the killing. It will be recalled that,
when Paul tells Annie that he intends to give Mrs Morel the
morphia, 'they both laughed together', and that their laughter is
described as the flickering of a 'little sanity': it suggests, then,
not only the tension they feel and their instinctive ('sane') need
for some relief from their oppressive horror, but also the sanity –
in defiance of established law – which the mercy-killing represents. They are also said, however, to laugh 'like two conspiring
children'. Taken together with the fact that Paul replies to
Annie's question in the dialect of his youth, the simile, I think,
points back to an earlier and apparently irrelevant incident
which illuminates the meaning of Paul's killing of his mother.

The only childhood 'conspiracy' in which Paul and Annie can be said to engage occurs when he decides to burn her doll, which he has accidentally smashed. The 'flickering' of Paul's 'sanity', it seems, should ultimately be related to the flames in which the doll is 'sacrificed':

'You couldn't tell it was there, mother; you couldn't tell it was there,' he repeated over and over. So long as Annie wept for the doll he sat helpless with misery. Her grief wore itself out. She forgave her brother – he was so much upset. But a day or two afterwards she was shocked.

'Let's make a sacrifice of Arabella,' he said. 'Let's burn her.'

She was horrified, yet rather fascinated. She wanted to see what the boy would do. He made an altar of bricks, pulled some of the shavings out of Arabella's body, put the waxen fragments into the hollow face, poured on a little paraffin, and set the whole thing alight. He watched with wicked satisfaction the drops of wax melt off the broken forehead of Arabella, and drop like sweat into the flame. So long as the stupid big doll burned he rejoiced in silence. At the end he poked among the embers with a stick, fished out the arms and legs, all blackened, and smashed them under stones.

'That's the sacrifice of Missis Arabella,' he said. 'An' I'm glad there's nothing left of her.'

Which disturbed Annie inwardly, although she could say nothing. He seemed to hate the doll so intensely, because he had broken it. (ch. IV)

Child psychologists, I imagine, would find the symbolism of this burning of the doll familiar. The 'wicked satisfaction' which Paul derives from his violent and compulsive destruction of the doll is surely not unrelated to the fact that he calls the 'big' doll 'Missis' Arabella and that the melted wax of its forehead drops 'like sweat' into the flame. But I am not so much concerned with the burning of the doll as an expression of a childhood wish to destroy the mother as with its relation to the actual killing which takes place later. First, we might note, in passing, the analogy between Paul's smashing of the arms and legs of the doll after the burning and his urge to smother his mother after she has already taken the morphia. Second, he hates and destroys the doll 'because he [has] broken it'; in other words, the 'sacrifice' represents some sort of expiation – as, in a measure, the killing is an unconscious purgation of the feelings of guilt which his ambiguous relationship with his mother has necessarily involved. Third, the burning of the doll seems to represent a childish but resolute refusal to sacrifice himself to it. In the same way, the killing, in one of its complex meanings, is a decisive protest against the self-sacrifice which subjection to his mother has entailed:

And he came back to her. And in his soul was a feeling of the satisfaction of self-sacrifice because he was faithful to her. She loved him first; he loved her first. And yet it was not enough. His new young life, so strong and imperious, was urged towards something else. It made him mad with restlessness. . . . (ch. ix)

Indeed, the pernicious effect of self-sacrifice is an insistent theme in the novel. Mrs Morel's married life is almost wholly self-sacrificial, involving as it does unwilling service of her husband, and despite her possessive love for Paul, abnegation of self for the sake of her children. In fact her self-sacrifice borders, masochistically, on the self-destructive:

'Are you sure it's a tumour?' [Paul asked Dr Ansell]. 'Why did Dr Jameson in Nottingham never find out anything about it? She's been going to him for weeks, and he's treated her for heart and indigestion.'
'Mrs Morel never told Dr Jameson about the lump,' said the doctor. (ch. xiii)

Mrs Morel is the embodiment of a principle which Lawrence fought against all his life, and in refusing to sacrifice himself to her, Paul repudiates a great deal of what she stands for. Nor is Paul's fight against self-sacrifice confined to his relations with his mother; it is also at the heart of his conflict with Miriam. It is perhaps significant that, of all the major characters, Walter Morel is the only one who doggedly pursues his own way, neither sacrificing himself for others nor expecting that they should sacrifice themselves for him.

*Sons and Lovers*, then, forcefully suggests Paul's ultimate rejection of his mother; it also implies his unconscious identification with his father. As far as his father is concerned, there are no dramatic manifestations of feeling comparable to his killing of his mother and his turning towards the town at the end of the book, but his identification with him is none the less unmistakable. It shows itself, for instance, in his unconscious imitation of his father's mannerisms – when Morel greets Clara she sees 'Paul's manner of bowing and shaking hands' (ch. XII) – and, more explicitly, in his reflections on class:

'You know,' he said to his mother, 'I don't want to belong to the well-to-do middle class. I like my common people best. I belong to the common people.'

'But if anyone else said so, my son, wouldn't you be in a tear. *You* know you consider yourself equal to any gentleman.'

'In myself,' he answered, 'not in my class or my education or my manners. But in myself I am.'

'Very well, then. Then why talk about the common people?'

'Because – the difference between people isn't in their class, but in themselves. Only from the middle classes one gets ideas, and from the common people – life itself, warmth. You feel their hates and loves.'

'It's all very well, my boy. But, then, why don't you go and talk to your father's pals?'

'But they're rather different.'

'Not at all. They're the common people. After all, whom do you mix with now – among the common people? Those that exchange ideas, like the middle classes. The rest don't interest you.'

'But – there's the life –'

'I don't believe there's a jot more life from Miriam than you could get from any educated girl – say Miss Moreton. It is *you* who are snobbish about class.' (ch. x)

Paul's ideas about class, it may be remarked, are a rough statement of the sort of clash which is dramatized in *Lady Chatterley's Lover*; they also point to the way in which he is drawn to his father. There is of course a lot in what Mrs Morel says, and Paul finds it difficult to define his feelings and to explain his reluctance to associate with his 'father's pals', but if he could bring himself to own it, it is clearly his father – and not Miriam, as Mrs Morel jealously and falsely supposes – who is the prototype of his image of the 'common people' (to whom he feels he belongs) and who embodies the vitality and exuberance and warmth which evokes his deepest sympathies. And despite his antipathy towards his father, he recognizes what it is that Morel has given his wife: the 'real, real flame of feeling' which he tells Miriam his mother has experienced 'through' his father (ch. XII) is simply an alternative phrase for 'life itself, warmth', for that quality which he tries to convince his mother the working class possesses.

I think it is fair to assume that the depiction of Paul's relations with his mother and father is a reliable guide to the nature of Lawrence's feelings about his own parents. Certainly there is wide agreement about his unconscious identification with his father in real life and in the work which follows *Sons and Lovers*. And Lawrence himself, though he phrases the affirmation obliquely, attests the vital nature of the bond which existed between him and his father:

. . . if the large parent mother-germ still lives and acts vividly and mysteriously in the great fused nucleus of your solar plexus, does the smaller, brilliant male-spark that derived from your father act any less vividly? By no means. It is different – it is less ostensible. It may be even in magnitude smaller. But it may be even more vivid, even more intrinsic. So beware how you deny the father-quick of yourself. You may be denying the most intrinsic quick of all.[13]

It is also instructive, I think, to compare the following two passages, the first from *Sons and Lovers*, the second from a letter written a few months after the completion of the novel:

Gertrude Coppard had watched [Morel], fascinated. He was so full of colour and animation, his voice ran so easily into comic grotesque, he was so ready and so pleasant with everybody. Her own father had a rich fund of humour, but it was satiric. This man's was different: soft, non-intellectual, warm, a kind of gambolling.

She herself was opposite. She had a curious, receptive mind, which found much pleasure and amusement in listening to other folk. She was clever in leading folk to talk. She loved ideas, and was considered very intellectual. What she liked most of all was an argument on religion or philosophy or politics with some educated man. . . .

She was a puritan, like her father, high-minded, and really stern. Therefore the dusky, golden softness of this man's sensuous flame of life, that flowed off his flesh like the flame from a candle, not baffled and gripped into incandescence by thought and spirit as her life was, seemed to her something wonderful, beyond her. (ch. 1)

I conceive a man's body as a kind of flame, like a candle flame, forever upright and yet flowing: and the intellect is just the light that is shed on to the things around. And I am not so much concerned with the things around – which is really mind – but with the mystery of the flame forever flowing, coming God knows how from out of practically nowhere, and being *itself*, whatever there is around it, that it lights up. . . .[14]

The recurrence of the striking candle flame image, with its suggestion of glowing warmth and mysterious being, signifies yet again a link between what Lawrence's father was (I think it is safe, at this stage, to identify the characters with their prototypes in real life) and what he himself was most concerned with. And it was not to his mother alone, we sense, that what the miner was 'seemed something wonderful'. But there are other implications to the passage quoted from the novel. What it vividly suggests is the strength of the impulse by which the young couple are attracted to their opposites, and the opposition described is so radical that it clearly must have had an important influence on Lawrence himself. Indeed Diana Trilling declares that, 'identifying himself now with the one parent, now with the other, Lawrence tried throughout his life to understand and to reconstitute in his own person their unhappy marriage',[15] and Richard Rees follows her in believing that Lawrence's 'attempt to balance the scale [of values represented by his parents] was to be an important part of his life's work'.[16] The views of these critics link up, at one point, with those advanced in Chapter 1 of this discussion, but the difference between us is precisely that which I wish to pursue in the analysis of Lawrence's development subsequent to the writing of *Sons and Lovers*. This seminal novel suggests the personal significance of Lawrence's formulation some two years later (in the Hardy essay) of the male and female principles. A comparison between the table in chapter 1[17] and the passage describing the meeting of his father and mother indicates that, in terms of that formulation, it is the decidedly male father who represents the *female* principle and the mother the *male*. (It is noticeable, even, that the '*golden* softness' of the miner's 'sensuous *flame* of life' is '*dusky*'.) Lawrence's formulation of the female principle as a complement of the male principle may therefore be viewed as an attempt to give full weight to qualities which his father embodied and which were underrated in his own home. Indeed the value accorded the female principle is a measure of his liberation from his mother's dominance. But the fact that his father is associated with the female principle and his mother with the male is also suggestive of the cause of the breach in his own nature. It is this breach which made it imperative for him to try to reconcile the opposing qualities within himself. The novels after *Sons and Lovers* are a record of this struggle and of the violent negations it engendered.

## NOTES

1. Letter to A. W. McLeod, Oct. 1913. [Extract reprinted on p. 26 of present volume. G.S.]

2. Cf. John Middleton Murry: '. . . it had been discovered that in *Sons and Lovers* Lawrence had independently arrived at the main conclusions of the psycho-analysts, and the English followers of Freud came to see him'. (*Reminiscences of D. H. Lawrence* (1933) p. 39.)

3. *Freudianism and the Literary Mind* (Baton Rouge, 1945) p. 153.

4. Letter dated 14 Nov. 1912. [Extract reprinted on p. 25 of present volume. G.S.]

5. 'D. H. Lawrence on Mother-Love', in *Essays in Criticism*, VIII (July 1958) 287.

6. Mark Schorer, 'Technique as Discovery'. [Reprinted on pp. 106–111 of the present volume. G.S.]

7. Helen Corke, *D. H. Lawrence's 'Princess': A Memory of Jessie Chambers* (Thames Ditton, 1951) p. 13.

8. A. L. Rowse, *The English Past* (1951) p. 230.

9. William York Tindall, *Forces in Modern British Literature, 1885–1956* (New York, 1956) pp. 222–3.

10. Eliseo Vivas, *D. H. Lawrence: The Failure and the Triumph of Art* (Evanston, 1960) p. 183. [Extract reprinted in the present volume on pp. 171–6. G.S.]

11. Anthony West, *D. H. Lawrence* (1950) pp. 14, 115.

12. Graham Hough. [See extract in the present volume on pp. 152–9. G.S.]

13. *Fantasia of the Unconscious* (New York, 1922; London, 1923) p. 24.

14. Letter to Ernest Collings, Jan. 1913.

15. 'Lawrence: Creator and Dissenter', in *The Saturday Review of Literature*, xxix (7 Dec. 1946) xviii.

16. *Brave Men: A Study of D. H. Lawrence and Simone Weil* (1958) p. 42.

17. This enumerates the attributes assigned by Lawrence to the 'male' and 'female' principles in the 'Study of Thomas Hardy'. G.S.

# Keith Sagar

# THE BASES OF THE NORMAL (1966)*

THE unnatural intensity, the clenched will of Miriam, relates her unmistakably to Hermione Roddice of *Women in Love*, even in its physical manifestation, a heaviness, almost a clumsiness in her movements:

Her body was not flexible and living. She walked with a swing, rather heavily, her head bowed forward, pondering. She was not clumsy, and yet none of her movements seemed quite *the* movement. Often, when wiping the dishes, she would stand in bewilderment and chagrin because she had pulled in two halves a cup or a tumbler. It was as if, in her fear and self-mistrust, she put too much strength into the effort. There was no looseness or abandon about her. Everything was gripped stiff with intensity, and her effort, overcharged, closed in on itself. (ch. VII)

We are reminded again of Mrs Morel:

Her movements were light and quick. It was always a pleasure to watch her. Nothing she ever did, no movement she ever made, could have been found fault with by her children. (ch. IV)

But, even more than it throws us back to Mrs Morel, this throws us forward to Clara:

She stood on top of the stile, and he held both her hands. Laughing, she looked down into his eyes. Then she leaped. Her breast came against his; he held her, and covered her face with kisses. (ch. XII)

The Miriam passage continues:

But she was physically afraid. If she were getting over a stile, she

* This extract has been slightly revised by the author for inclusion in the present volume. G.S.

gripped his hands in a little hard anguish, and began to lose her presence of mind. And he could not persuade her to jump from even a small height. Her eyes dilated, became exposed and palpitating. 'No!' she cried, half laughing in terror – 'no!'

'You shall!' he once cried, and, jerking her forward, he brought her falling from the fence. But her wild 'Ah!' of pain, as if she were losing consciousness, cut him. (ch. VII)

The same physical inhibition prevents Miriam from enjoying the swing. This episode is characteristic of the novel – remarkable for its realism and freshness, embodying resources far greater than those needed for mere presentation, resources which serve to relate the episode closely to the overall structure of the novel and to invest it with a deeper moral significance.

Paul swings 'like a bird that swings for joy of movement'; he finds it 'a treat of a swing – a real treat of a swing'. Miriam is amazed that he takes his enjoyment so seriously. But for Paul life is made up of such moments of intensity, an intensity as relaxed and whole as hers is taut and unbalanced, moments when the body is given over to something outside the will, in this case the rhythm of the swing:

She could feel him falling and lifting through the air, as if he were lying on some force. . . . For the moment he was nothing but a piece of swinging stuff: not a particle of him that did not swing. (ch. VII)

Miriam is roused watching him:

It were almost as if he were a flame that had lit a warmth in her whilst he swung in the middle air. (ch. VII)

Mrs Morel had been able to yield to joy, to Walter's 'flame of life', but Miriam 'cannot lose herself so'. When her turn comes she grips the rope with fear, resisting the forces which seek to carry her. The sexual implication is clear in the hot waves of fear through her bowels which accompany Paul's rhythmic thrusts. The fiasco of their eventual consummation could be predicted from this scene.

Miriam's reluctance to give herself up to life, and, more specifically, to put herself in the hands of the man she loves, contrasts, again, with Clara:

'Will you go down to the river?' he asked.

She looked at him, leaving herself in his hands. He went over the brim of the declivity and began to climb down.

'It is slippery', he said.

'Never mind', she replied.

The red clay went down almost sheer. He slid, went from one tuft of grass to the next, hanging on to the bushes, making for a little platform at the foot of a tree. There he waited for her, laughing with excitement. Her shoes were clogged with red earth. It was hard for her. He frowned. At last he caught her hand, and she stood beside him. The cliff rose above them and fell away below. Her colour was up, her eyes flashed. He looked at the big drop below them.

'It's risky', he said; 'or messy, at any rate. Shall we go back?'

'Not for my sake', she said quickly. . . .

She was coming perilously down.

'Mind!' he warned her. He stood with his back to the tree, waiting.

'Come now', he called, opening his arms.

She let herself run. He caught her, and together they stood watching the dark water scoop at the raw edge of the bank. (ch. XII)

Clara's natural abandon makes their first intimacy easy for Paul, despite the hazards. Afterwards, glowing with happiness, they go for tea in the village. An old lady presents Clara with 'three tiny dahlias in full blow, neat as bees, and speckled scarlet and white' (ch. XII). The offering is made 'because we were jolly', Paul tells Miriam.

Flower themes are woven into the whole novel so skilfully that only cumulatively does one recognise their symbolism. A scene in the first chapter identifies Mrs Morel with the flowers, and, through them, with all the mysterious potentialities of life:

She became aware of something about her. With an effort she roused herself to see what it was that penetrated her consciousness. The tall white lilies were reeling in the moonlight, and the air was charged with their perfume as with a presence. Mrs Morel gasped slightly in fear. She touched the big, pallid flowers on their petals, then shivered. They seemed to be stretching in the moonlight. She put her hand into one white bin: the gold scarcely showed on her fingers by moonlight. She bent down to look at the binful of yellow pollen; but it only appeared dusky. Then she drank a deep draught of the scent. It almost made her dizzy. (ch. 1)

She is pregnant with Paul, and it is stressed that this communion is shared by the unborn child. The night she looks out on is not only nature, it is all that the infinite distance offers:

The night was very large, and very strange, stretching its hoary distances infinitely. And out of the silver-grey fog of darkness came sounds vague and hoarse: a corncrake not far off, sound of a train like a sigh, and distant shouts of men. (ch. 1)

The symbolic character of the passage is underlined on the following page, when Mrs Morel, looking in the mirror, smiles to see 'her face all smeared with the yellow dust of lilies'. The night into which Mrs Morel here merges is moonlit, shiny, hoary, silver-grey, rich with scents and sounds and the dusky gold of the pollen. And Paul is here baptised into life.

At the structural centre of the novel, at the critical moment when Paul rejects Miriam finally for Clara, there is a second night-communion which in part repeats, in part subtly qualifies and extends, the symbolism of the first. The lilies are now described as madonna lilies:

Through the open door, stealthily, came the scent of madonna lilies, almost as if it were prowling abroad. (ch. xi)

We remember from the earlier scene the overpowering perfume, the streaming white light of the full moon, the whiteness of all the flowers. In the later scene there is a half-moon, dusky gold, which makes the sky dull purple, and which disappears below the hill at the very moment when Paul catches 'another perfume, something raw and coarse':

Hunting round, he found the purple iris, touched their fleshy throats and their dark, grasping hands. At any rate he had found something. (ch. XI)

The next chapter is called 'Passion'. The intense whiteness of the full moon and the lilies, formerly a condition of Paul's growth within an all-encompassing mother-love, is now becoming a weight upon him, a 'barrier' to his further maturing. The blanched white light is the possession of his soul by women who, as mother and virgin, cannot foster the life of the body and the development of a strong, self-sufficient masculinity.

As the first night-communion gave a blessing to the unborn child, so the second blesses the new self which is coming into being within Paul:

Often, as he talked to Clara Dawes, came that thickening and quickening of his blood, that peculiar concentration in the breast, as if something were alive there, a new self, or a new centre of consciousness. (ch. IX)

The new self responds to Clara impersonally, as a woman rather than a person, almost physiologically. And Mrs Morel approves: 'At any rate that feeling was wholesome.' She even invites Clara to Sunday tea:

Clara felt she completed the circle, and it was a pleasure to her. But she was rather afraid of the self-possession of the Morels, father and all. She took their tone; there was a feeling of balance. It was a cool, clear atmosphere, where everyone was himself, and in harmony. . . . Miriam realised that Clara was accepted as she had never been. (ch. XII)

Mrs Morel's verdict is confirmed by the novel:

'Yes, I liked her. But you'll tire of her my son; you know you will.' (ch. XII)

The consummation with Clara is wonderfully done. The significance of the experience is conveyed largely in the symbolism of the Trent in flood:

The Trent was very full. It swept silent and insidious under the bridge, travelling in a soft body. There had been a great deal of rain. On the river levels were flat gleams of flood water. The sky was grey, with glisten of silver here and there. . . . There was the faintest haze over the silvery-dark water and the green meadow bank, and the elm-trees that were spangled with gold. The river slid by in a body, utterly silent and swift, intertwining among itself like some subtle, complex creature. . . . Sometimes there below they caught glimpses of the full, soft-sliding Trent, and of water-meadows dotted with small cattle. . . . The far-below water-meadows were very green. He and she stood leaning against one another, silent, afraid, their bodies touching all along. There came a quick gurgle from the river below. (ch. XII)

There is more here than a mere water-equals-fertility symbol. The splashes of silver and gold remind us of the positives of the night-communions. The Trent is the great surge of uninhibited instinct, emotion, which carries all before it:

As a rule, when he started love-making, the emotion was strong enough to carry with it everything – reason, soul, blood – in a great sweep, like the Trent carries bodily its back-swirls and intertwinings, noiselessly. Gradually the little criticisms, the little sensations, were lost, thought also went, everything borne along in one flood. He became, not a man with a mind, but a great instinct. (ch. XIII)

The abstraction of his relationship with Miriam – 'his natural fire of love . . . transmitted into the fine stream of thought' – had cut him off from life. Clara puts him in touch again:

Just as he was, so it seemed the vigorous wintry stars were strong also with life. He and they struck with the same pulse of fire, and the same joy of strength which held the bracken-frond stiff near his eyes held his own body firm. (ch. XIII)

Throughout the novel, this faculty for being in touch with life has been stressed in Paul, and its absence in Miriam. It is a matter of respect for the unique otherness of phenomena, the mythic faculty of meeting phenomena in an I–thou relationship, meeting but not merging, as Miriam seeks to do, which is a violation of

individuality. The impersonality of sex particularly horrifies
Miriam:

He seemed to be almost unaware of her as a person: she was only
to him then a woman. She was afraid. . . . This thick-voiced,
oblivious man was a stranger to her. (ch. XI)

He comes to Clara in the same way, and she too is frightened.
But ultimately she does not mind being 'only' a woman. She
realises that a woman is more than a person, and this realisation
gives her access to a depth of religious experience unknown to
Miriam:

The naked hunger and inevitability of his loving her, something
strong and blind and ruthless in its primitiveness, made the hour
almost terrible to her. She knew how stark and alone he was, and
she felt it was great that he came to her; and she took him simply
because his need was bigger either than her or him, and her soul
was still within her. (ch. XIII)

It is through the very strangeness of the woman that Paul gains
access to the darkness which is both the unknown forces and
purposes of the wheeling universe, and the equally unknown
forces and purposes deep within himself:

All the while the peewits were screaming in the field. When he
came to, he wondered what was near his eyes, curving and
strong with life in the dark, and what voice it was speaking. Then
he realised it was the grass, and the peewit was calling. The
warmth was Clara's breathing heaving. He lifted his head, and
looked into her eyes. They were dark and shining and strange,
life wild at the source staring into his life, stranger to him, yet
meeting him; and he put his face down on her throat, afraid.
What was she? A strong, strange, wild life, that breathed with his
in the darkness through this hour. It was all so much bigger than
themselves that he was hushed. They had met, and included in
their meeting the thrust of the manifold grass stems, the cry of
the peewit, the wheel of the stars. (ch. XIII)

From now on in Lawrence's work, life is not to be judged by
merely human standards; rather, human values are themselves

exposed to standards drawn from experiences and relationships in an animistic universe:

To know their own nothingness, to know the tremendous living flood which carried them always, gave them rest within themselves. If so great a magnificent power could overwhelm them, identify them altogether with itself, so that they knew that they were only grains in the tremendous heave that lifted every grass blade its little height, and every tree, and living thing, then why fret about themselves? They could let themselves be carried by life, and they felt a sort of peace, each in the other. There was a verification which they had had together. Nothing could nullify it, nothing could take it away; it was almost their belief in life. (ch. XIII)

It is this faith which finally saves Paul from the temptation to merge with the dying mother into the other darkness, of death. Clara has now taken over from the mother the initiation of Paul into life.

But the Trent imagery has also suggested the limitations of this passion; like floodwaters, it is something beyond control, accumulated and unresolved, unless it takes its place in a whole human relationship which Paul finds impossible with Clara.

I cannot see what prevents a permanent relationship between Paul and Clara. The ease with which they are so shortly to separate leaves rather high and dry these powerful affirmative passages. I would not be surprised to find that these passages were new in the final 1912 version, and drew their power from Lawrence's relationship with Frieda. Lawrence was probably strongly tempted to make Clara into a Frieda figure, but realised that the novel as it stood could not accommodate such potent new material, but must end with the death of the mother and Paul alone in the world. It might have been better for the unity of the novel if the love-making with Clara had yielded intimations rather than such confident affirmations of life.

*Laurence Lerner*

# BLOOD AND MIND: THE FATHER
# IN *SONS AND LOVERS* (1967)

THROUGH the whole of Lawrence runs a contrast between two kinds of men. It is something like Hardy's contrast between the gentleman and the peasant, but more defiant, more violent, more deep-searching. On the one hand, there are men like the younger Tom Brangwen (Ursula's uncle) and Skrebensky in *The Rainbow*, Dr Mitchell in *The Lost Girl*, Rico in *St Mawr*, the vicar in *The Virgin and the Gipsy*, Mr Massey in 'The Daughters of the Vicar', Owen in *The Plumed Serpent*, and Clifford Chatterley. These men are sophisticated, spiteful, often intellectuals, often rich, and always against life. On the other hand are Morel in *Sons and Lovers*: Cicio in *The Lost Girl*, the two grooms in *St Mawr* (Lewis more than Phoenix, and neither of them fully, for the character who really belongs here is the horse itself), the gipsy in *The Virgin and the Gipsy*, Arthur in 'The Daughters of the Vicar', both Ramon and Cipriano in *The Plumed Serpent*, and Mellors. These men are often working class, sometimes foreign, full of a smouldering, sullen energy, impulsive, unintellectual, contemptuous of reasonings, and highly sexed.

Looking at these lists (both of which could be much longer, especially if we included the tales) we must be struck with one thought: that with a single exception, they do not show Lawrence at his best. For this contrast, that Lawrence draws over and over again, is a contrast to do with phallic worship: he draws it in order to assert his doctrine, and in it he does not, or not often, speak the speech of art, the 'only true speech'.

'Yes, I will come,' he said, still watching the bicycle tube, which sprawled nakedly on the floor. The forward drop of his head was curiously beautiful to her, the straight, powerful nape of the neck, the delicate shape of the back of the head, the black hair.

The way the neck sprang from the strong loose shoulders was beautiful. There was something mindless but *intent* about the forward reach of his head. His face seemed colourless, neutral-tinted and expressionless.[1]

That is not the speech of art, it is a mechanical doling out of Lawrentian phrases (above all, 'mindless but *intent*'). Cicio has not been seen, we have nothing but an assertion of his power, of the fact that he stands for a force of life in the book. And how the doughy, dull presentation of Cicio contrasts with the vivid reality of the Houghtons and the world of Woodhouse.

I said there was one exception to this: and that of course is Morel. Lawrence hardly ever created a character more convincing, more coherent (without being merely predictable) and more alive than this version of the father he resented and regarded as having dragged his mother down. To illustrate the power with which Morel is created one would need to quote the whole book, but I will mention two episodes in particular. One is the birth of Paul. Mrs Morel (who has a hard time) is helped by a neighbour, Mrs Bower; the baby is born while Morel is at work and he returns, tired, hungry and dirty, to find a strange woman in possession:

Morel, thinking nothing, dragged his way up the garden path, wearily and angrily. He closed his umbrella, and stood it in the sink; then he sluthered his heavy boots into the kitchen. Mrs Bower appeared in the inner doorway.

'Well,' she said, 'she's about as bad as she can be. It's a boy childt.'

The miner grunted, put his empty snap-bag and his tin bottle on the dresser, went back into the scullery and hung up his coat, then came and dropped into his chair.

'Han yer got a drink?' he asked.

The woman went into the pantry. There was heard the pop of a cork. She set the mug, with a little, disgusted rap, on the table before Morel. He drank, gasped, wiped his big moustache on the end of his scarf, drank, gasped, and lay back in his chair. The woman would not speak to him again. She set his dinner before him, and went upstairs. (ch. II)

If sympathy lies anywhere in this scene, it is surely with the man. Lawrence is showing us the sex war, and it is the woman (as so often on occasions of childbirth) who is the aggressor. Morel is completely self-centred, but he has the excuse of exhaustion; Mrs Bower is concerned about Mrs Morel but, we see here, in a way that uses sympathy as fuel for indignation: instead of her anger with Morel being the consequence of her concern for his wife, the concern almost exists to feed the anger. And all of this is conveyed in that one completely apt physical detail, the 'little, disgusted rap' of the mug on the table – too actual for a symbol, but enclosing in itself the whole meaning of the incident.

In the very next incident, we see another side of Morel. He returns home to find the Congregational clergyman having tea in the house:

> Morel took off his coat, dragged his armchair to table, and sat down heavily.
> 'Are you tired?' asked the clergyman.
> 'Tired? I ham that,' replied Morel. '*You* don't know what it is to be tired, as *I'm* tired.'
> 'No,' replied the clergyman.
> 'Why, look yer 'ere,' said the miner, showing the shoulders of his singlet. 'It's a bit dry now, but it's wet as a clout with sweat even yet. Feel it.'
> 'Goodness!' cried Mrs Morel. 'Mr Heaton doesn't want to feel your nasty singlet.'
> The clergyman put out his hand gingerly. (ch. 11)

Once again, what we must notice is the perfect truth of the scene, the sharpness with which Lawrence has seen everyone's behaviour – so sharply that in its last detail the passage is almost comic. The sympathy we were offered for Morel is hovering again as the scene begins: Mrs Morel's exclamation is a token of her alienation from his habits, so automatic that she cannot be blamed, but none the less cruel. But when Morel comes in he forfeits it all by dramatising his position, enjoying his moral advantage over the clergyman in exactly the same way Mrs Bower had enjoyed hers over him.

It is a sign of Lawrence's mastery that in so short a space he can show us Morel in two such different lights, and convince us that they are not merely compatible but complementary, that the man who behaved in one way is likely to behave in the other. Both these scenes come early in the book, but the character of Morel continues to develop and to be explored, even until he is an old man, no longer in the foreground, tamed by age and still under Lawrence's scrutiny.

In later life Lawrence confessed that he thought he had been unjust to his father, and said that if he were to write the book again he would be more sympathetic to the father, and less to the mother. How thankful we can be that he never did this! For it cannot be coincidence that Morel, the most successful of Lawrence's surly sexed and vital men, is the one against whom he bears a grudge: it is that grudge which stiffened Lawrence's treatment of him, caused him to see Morel with ruthless clarity, and kept away the indulgence and hysteria that caused Lawrence to ruin so many other versions of such a character (and whose seeds no doubt were already present in what gave Morel his vitality). The resentment is, of course, personal in origin: Lawrence hates Morel because it is his father. From this we can conclude that here is an author who writes better, not worse, for incompletely detaching himself from an autobiographical situation. When Lawrence made his recantation he had perhaps detached himself enough from his memories to feel calmly about his father; but that calmness would merely have laid Morel open to the forces in Lawrence that would have wanted to make him another Cicio, another Annable.

The reason why this contrast between two kinds of men recurs so regularly is that it is a sign of the very contrast with which we began: that between blood and mind. This can be used as a guide through Lawrence's fiction in other ways than as a method of sorting out the characters. If we ask ourselves what these violently committed books are asking us to accept and reject, we will find that we are indicating the full range of human experience that he covers. And we can express our disquiet by saying that there is too much in what he rejects that is admirable, even necessary, too much in what he accepts that is pernicious. What he rejects is too like reason, what he accepts is too like brutality.


## NOTE

1. *The Lost Girl*, ch. VIII.

# QUESTIONS

1. What light does either Lawrence's original Foreword (p. 30) or his letter to Garnett of 14 November 1912 (p. 24) cast on *Sons and Lovers*?

2. Compare the view of art and of the relationship of the artist to society in *Sons and Lovers* and Joyce's *Portrait of the Artist as a Young Man*.

3. 'It's the end of my youthful period?' How true, in retrospect, is Lawrence's own comment on the novel?

4. 'I shan't write in the same manner as *Sons and Lovers* again, I think – in that hard, violent style full of sensation and presentation.' Has Lawrence characterized the style of the novel accurately?

5. Using the letter to Barbara Low (pp. 26–7) as a guide, attempt to set out in some detail what you consider Lawrence's objections to the 'psycho-analytic' view of his novel (and/or of the world).

6. Does the value of *Sons and Lovers* depend wholly or mainly on the validity of the theory of the Oedipus complex? Is it possible to make a case for the novel even on the assumption that the theory is false?

7. How acute is Lawrence as a critic of industrial society?

8. Is it possible to identify Paul Morel entirely with the author? What signs are there *in the novel itself* (rather than in extraneous biographical data) that 'Paul Morel' is *not* the author of *Sons and Lovers*?

9. What is the attitude to Walter Morel which emerges from the early part of the novel?

10. Has *Sons and Lovers* any real unity as a novel, or is it at least two separate novels co-existing uneasily in a single book?

11. How far is it true that *Sons and Lovers* and autobiographical novels like it, written in the first half of the twentieth century, 'are rooted in the modern emancipation of women'? (Alfred Kazin)

12. Consider the different uses to which Lawrence puts the same raw material in the 'Miriam' and 'Mother' poems, the play *A Collier's Friday Night* and *Sons and Lovers*. What conclusions, if any, would you draw about the relationship between art and reality?

13. Where does the novel place the blame for the breakdown of the Paul–Miriam relationship? On Paul? On Miriam? On the mother? Is the author, in your view, fully aware of all the tensions and pressures in this triangular relationship?

14. If Lawrence had written only *Sons and Lovers*, would he still be an important figure in English literature?

# SELECT BIBLIOGRAPHY

Many of Lawrence's own writings are very useful in enlarging our understanding of *Sons and Lovers* and the cultural and emotional milieu from which it arose. Apart from the letters and poems included in this volume, there are several other letters of this period as well as many poems dealing with his relations with his mother and the perpetual strife between his parents ('Monologue of a Mother' and 'Discord in Childhood', for example). The long essay 'Nottingham and the Mining Country' and the play *A Collier's Friday Night* should also be read.

Among the critical essays not included here, Alfred Kazin's Introduction to the American Modern Library edition (Random House, 1962) and Louis Fraiberg's 'The Unattainable Self' (in *Twelve Original Essays on Great English Novels*, ed. Charles Shapiro (Wayne State U.P., 1960)) are well worth looking at. For the reader interested in the book's Freudian connections, apart from Fraiberg's essay referred to above, there is Frederick Hoffman's essay 'Lawrence's Quarrel with Freud' (in *Freudianism and the Literary Mind* (Louisiana State U.P., 1957) and, more comprehensive and formidable, *Oedipus in Nottingham* by Daniel A. Weiss (University of Washington Press, 1962). Other useful essays will be found in Mark Spilka's *The Love Ethic of D. H. Lawrence* (Indiana U.P., 1955; Dobson, 1958) and Julian Moynahan's *The Deed of Life* (Oxford U.P. and Princeton U.P., 1963). Gāmini Salgādo's short study of *Sons and Lovers* (Arnold, 1966) is a straightforward attempt at a critical account of the impact of the novel as one reads it.

The definitive life of Lawrence is Edward Nehls' three-volume composite biography (University of Wisconsin Press, 1957–9). There are two shorter but quite reliable studies by Harry T.

Moore, *The Life and Works of D. H. Lawrence* (Twayne and Allen & Unwin, 1951) and *The Intelligent Heart* (Heinemann, 1955; also available in Penguin paperback). The standard bibliography is in the Soho Bibliographies series (Hart-Davies, 1963) and is edited by Warren Roberts. *Modern Fiction Studies*, v (Spring 1959) i, contains a useful checklist of Lawrence criticism, as does Keith Sagar's *The Art of D. H. Lawrence* (Cambridge U.P., 1966).

# NOTES ON CONTRIBUTORS

MAURICE BEEBE, author of *Ivory Towers and Sacred Founts* and editor of *Modern Fiction Studies*, is Professor of English at Purdue University.

SEYMOUR BETSKY, American critic, teaches English at Utrecht University, Holland. He is a former contributor to *Scrutiny*.

DAVID DAICHES, author of over twenty critical works, is Dean of the School of English and American Studies at the University of Sussex.

H. M. DALESKI teaches English at the Hebrew University of Jerusalem. *The Forked Flame* is his first book of criticism.

GRAHAM HOUGH has published a volume of poetry and several critical works including studies of Yeats, the Romantics and *The Faerie Queene*. He is a fellow of Christ's College, Cambridge, and Professor of English.

LAURENCE LERNER, who teaches at the University of Sussex, has published two volumes of poetry, two volumes of criticism and two novels, the latest of which is entitled *A Free Man*.

SIMON LESSER, who has worked as research associate at the University of Chicago and New York Psychiatric Institutes and at the Washington School of Psychiatry, teaches English at Amherst College.

J. MIDDLETON MURRY, who died in 1957, was at one time a close associate of Lawrence. In addition to *Son of Woman*, he also wrote *Reminiscences of D. H. Lawrence* and several other more strictly critical works, including *The Problem of Style* and *Keats and Shakespeare*.

FRANK O'CONNOR is the best-known and one of the best of twentieth-century Irish short-story writers. He died in 1966.

KEITH SAGAR is author of a doctoral dissertation on D. H. Lawrence for Leeds University, and is Resident Tutor in North-East Lancashire for the Extra-Mural Department of Manchester University.

MARK SCHORER, Professor of English at Berkeley, University of California, is the author of several critical articles, as well as a study of Blake and a biography of Sinclair Lewis. He is also a novelist.

DOROTHY VAN GHENT taught English at the University of Buffalo until her death in 1967.

ELISEO VIVAS is Professor of Philosophy at Northwestern University and has published several articles on aesthetic problems. He is the author of *Creation and Discovery*.

# INDEX